LIMN NUMBER FOUR
FOOD INFRASTRUCTURES
Edited by **Mikko Jauho, David Schleifer, Bart Penders and Xaq Frohlich**

PREFACE:
Food Infrastructures

XAQ FROHLICH,
MIKKO JAUHO,
BART PENDERS,
and **DAVID SCHLEIFER**
January, 2014

CONSIDER THE DIFFERENCE BETWEEN CATCHING A FISH AND buying fish fingers at your neighborhood supermarket. We may fail miserably at catching a fish, but we can easily imagine how to do so. But what does it take to enable the act of buying fish fingers? What processes has a product gone through before it arrives as food in our shopping basket or on our plates? Who are the millions of people at work in these processes, and what systems do they operate to keep us reliably provisioned with fish fingers?

This issue of *Limn* analyzes food infrastructures and addresses scale in food production, provision, and consumption. We aim to move beyond the tendency towards simple producer "push" or consumer "pull" accounts of the food system, focusing instead on the work that connects producers to consumers. By describing and analyzing food infrastructures, our contributors examine the reciprocal relationships among consumer choice, personal use, and the socio-material arrangements that enable, channel, and constrain our everyday food options.

FOOD SYSTEMS AS INFRASTRUCTURE
When we think of "infrastructure," what usually come to mind are roads, electricity grids, telephone lines, and water pipes. Not surprisingly, the growing body of research on large technological systems and infrastructures has mostly focused on electricity, water supply, communications, and transportation. But what insights can be gained when systems of food production, provision, and consumption are approached as an infrastructure?
Infrastructures are those invisible, unappreciated, and often mundane arrangements that support the carrying out of everyday tasks. For example, shopping for food typically involves a retail space with a characteristic internal organization and products of standardized content, size, and packaging. Only when the organization is changed, or a desired product is missing, does the arrangement become visible to consumers. But infrastructures are visible to those who operate them. And they are exceptionally visible to end-users when they fail because they are essential to the smooth operation of society. They create conditions for economic activity, produce collective security, and introduce reliability and predictability into the world. In this sense they are vital systems, indispensable to the reproduction of contemporary forms of life and indeed to life itself. This also makes them vulnerable and in need of protection. The availability of food and its efficient distribution to the population is a case in point: nations typically have in place elaborate plans to ensure national primary agricultural production and food provision in times of crisis.

The various contributions to this issue indicate how food systems resemble and interact with other vital infrastructures like water, electricity, and transportation. However, the food system also differ from those other infrastructures. One example is its relation to markets. In many places, water, gas, and electricity have a long-standing status as semi-public goods only recently privatized and opened up to market competition. Food provision appears more thoroughly structured by markets and market devices.

But food infrastructures are not limited to market activity. They are undergirded by invisible systems of state funds and by overt expressions of hunger and pleasure. Foods are targeted to nationally and demographically specific market segments even as they constantly move across geographic regions. Individuals and families continuously purchase and prepare food within households while long-term continuities across lifespans, cultures, and millennia shape what we eat for breakfast. Corporations operate production and delivery systems quickly enough to beat microbial growth and catch fashion cycles while corporations themselves grow, persevere, morph and die.

INFRASTRUCTURE AS SCALE

Infrastructures are also about scale. Producing food for oneself or one's family, storing it, and eating it requires a modest amount of external interference, input, or inward and outward flow of materials and knowledge. But producing foods for a few dozen or a few billion people is a different matter. Foods produced on larger scales must be predictable in quality, quantity, content, safety, cost, flavor, texture and return on investment. Achieving that predictability requires many specific modes of organizing and creating the world: viable and authoritative standards, distribution models, labeling protocols, safety guidelines, business models marketing and end-users. Hence, infrastructures are composed not only of physical artifacts and natural resources, but also human labor, forms of knowledge, laws and decrees, organizations and institutions, tastes and interests. Together, these elements make the food infrastructures that feed us all and that are featured in this issue.

INFRASTRUCTURE AS ANALYSIS

The authors in this issue of *Limn* use infrastructure to analyze food production, provision, and consumption. This approach enables the authors to look beyond consumer choice or business intentions and foreground the often invisible and implicit assumptions inscribed into the food system. Infrastructures embody tacit conventions of need and entitlement, which have a self-fulfilling character. They carry conceptions of proper use, thus inscribing a certain end-user or consumer. And because power is an outcome of establishing and operating the elements of an infrastructure, there are inherent ethical and political dimensions to food infrastructures and their study. Infrastructure as an analytic approach therefore offers a way to understand and critique the world of "Big Food," which is simultaneously varied and monolithic, indispensable and frightening.

Managing risk, avoiding disruption, nourishing families, and transmitting pleasure are sites of economic activity and also of governance, security, identity, morality, and mortality. This issue of *Limn* features contributions from a variety of scholars and practitioners devoted to transforming our understanding of food and of infrastructure, making us think twice as we traverse food production, procurement, preparation and consumption.

limn is published as needed. This issue is set using Christian Schwartz' Graphik and Dino dos Santos' Leitura typefaces. Layout by **Martin Hoyem/American Ethnography**. The General Editors of Limn are **Stephen J. Collier, Christopher M. Kelty**, and **Andrew Lakoff**. Issue No. 4 Editors: **Mikko Jauho, David Schleifer, Bart Penders, Xaq Frohlich** || This magazine copyright © 2014 the Editors and Martin Hoyem. All articles herein are copyright © 2014 by their respective authors. This magazine may not be reproduced without permission, however the articles are available online at http://limn.it/ and available for unrestricted use under a Creative Commons 3.0 unported License, http://creativecommons.org/licenses/by-sa/3.0/ || Cover Image: US Patent #7156635B2 "Multi-layer food product system and process" || Copyediting: **Michelle L. Treviño** (michelle.trevino@gmail.com) || Publication assistance provided by the Institute for Society and Genetics, University of California, Los Angeles. More at http://limn.it/

Elements of Food Infrastructure

Daily bread: Throughout recorded history, food has been one of the most enduring limitations shaping the templates and tenor of humankind's daily life. Civilization is virtually defined by finding it, securing it, and ensuring its future potential. "The countryside lived off its harvest and cities off the surplus," Braudel writes, and so it was that the geography of civilization's expanse had been marked by the security of sustenance close at hand. As food has industrialized, it has changed, along with our bodies and our economies. **Matthew Hockenberry** charts elements of the conceptual connections amongst the articles in this issue.

1650s–1680s
A Taste for Luxury →

The first coffeehouses spread from the Muslim world to major centers of European and Neo-European trade. Tea is introduced to England through the marriage of Charles II to the Portuguese princess Catherine of Braganza.
Taste • Transport • Consumer culture

1803
← The Cold Chain

Maryland farmer Thomas Moore first introduces the term refrigerator in an 1803 patent to describe the site of artificial cooling, new techniques for keeping things cold begin to infiltrate in the meatpacking and brewing industries over the course of the century.
Transport • Perishability • Architecture.

1809
↓ Tin Can Archaeologies

Nicholas Appert collected a 12,000 franc prize from Napoleon in 1809 for developing a means of keeping foods fresh without relying on foraging. Across the channel the British merchant Peter Durand set sail with boiled meats and soups sealed in his tin coated iron canisters, the Royal Navy was stocked with the future fuel of expansion, conflict, and colonization.
Storage • Transport • Perishability
Cochoy p20, Faber-Cullen p39

1871
Crimes Against Butter ↓

New York based United States Dairy Company begins controversial production of oleomargarine as a kind of "artificial butter" in 1871. By 1902 over thirty states had passed outright bans on the sale of colored oleomargarine and scores of violators had seen the inside of federal penitentiaries for unauthorized production.
Regulation • Health • Labeling
Jauho p36, Frohlich p42, Penders/Flipse p54

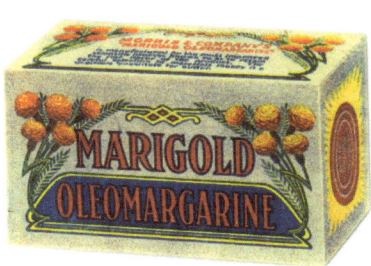

1906

Pigs' Lips and Assholes ↓

When Upton Sinclair's publication of *The Jungle* in 1906 brought not, as he had hoped, empathy with the plight of the immigrant worker, but public furor over the unsanitary conditions of food production, it opened a century of constant investigation into the composition of food.
Safety • Regulation
Freidberg p24, Yates-Doerr p32

1912

↑ Grocers in the Country Village, Grocers in the Great Town

The Great Atlantic & Pacific Tea Company (A&P) had begun as a mail order tea business in the middle of the nineteenth century. When it moved to systematic grocery distribution in 1912, its "economy store" brought standardization—and scale—through vertical integration over the distribution chain.
Safety • Taste • Consumer culture
Cochoy p20, Powell p50

1913

The Lipid Hypothesis →

When Nikolay Anichkov produced atherosclerosis in rabbits by feeding them cholesterol in 1913, the first intuitions of peril began to trickle into the work of scientists and doctors exploring the role of nutrition in human health.
Health • Consumer culture
Jauho p36, Hendrickx p14

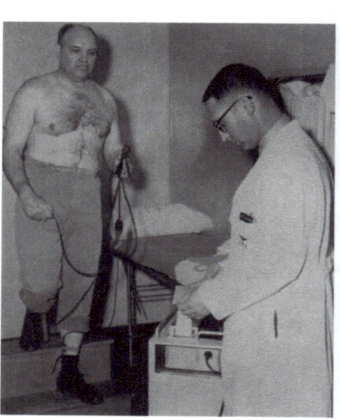

1920s

Monoculture →

In the early 1920s bananas had become the first exotic fruit commonly available to Americans leading to a near complete reconfiguration of places like Hondoruas by emergent multinationals like United Fruit.
Taste • Consumer culture
Paxson p28, Faber-Cullen p39,
Schleifer-Fairbrother p17

1930

The Center Store →

Michael Cullen pioneers developments like grocery carts to encourage bulk purchasing and a "center store," loaded with aisle after aisle of packaged national brands.
Architecture · Consumer culture
Powell p50, Cochoy p20

1938

The Food, Drug, and Cosmetic Act

lays the foundation for information about food in the United States by requiring that standards safeguard consumer value.
Information · Labeling · Safety
Frohlich p42, Penders/Flipse p54

1974

← Beep

The first bar code scanner is installed in a Marsh supermarket in Ohio
Information · Consumer culture
Powell p50.

1980

Food Networks →

Food conglomerates and industry groups retain A.D. Little to report on implementations of Electronic Data Interchange in the grocery industry—the foundational mechanisms for the supplier and distribution network of the modern chain grocery.
Information · Transport · Architecture
Dubuisson-Quellier p11, Powell p50, Freidberg p24

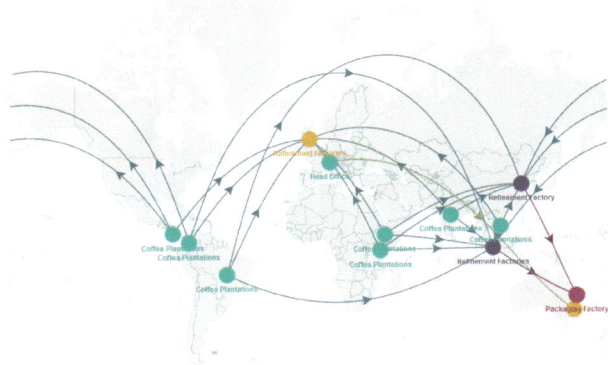

1990

The Nutrition Fact

The Nutrition Labeling and Education Act universalizes implementation of a nutrition label for all packaged foods, giving consumers the information to take responsibility for nutrition decisions.
Information · Labeling · Health
Frohlich p42, Penders/Flipse p54

1990

The Cradle to the Grave

At the first SETAC (Society of Environmental Toxicology and Chemistry) sponsored international workshop in 1990, the term "life cycle assessment" (LCA) is coined.
Safety · Transport
Freidberg p24, Lappé p58, Schleifer-Fairbrother p17

The Future

While the nineteenth and twentieth centuries had been defined by an increasing distance from the production of food, the twenty-first strives to reintegrate it. Hybrid categorizations of food production, composition, and consumption seems sure to proliferate with uncertain meanings, even as these meanings move to the forefront of consumptive choice and consumer concern.

[For the complete timeline by Matthew Hockenberry, see http://limn.it/]

SCALE, EVOLUTION AND EMERGENCE IN FOOD SYSTEMS

Christopher Otter diagnoses the impossibility of fully governing large-scale food systems and the novel ecologies they create.

an ecosystem, however small, is ultimately a food system, as Fritjof Capra has observed (Capra 2005:34). Among the most significant ecological effects of human populations has been the stretching of food systems across great tracts of space. Human beings have been doing this for centuries, even millennia, as the Roman grain trade, the spice trade, and the Columbian exchange demonstrate. Thus, large-scale food systems are not historically novel. Nonetheless, the past 200 years or so has seen a significant material transformation in how food is produced, processed, stored, and distributed. Food systems have become truly globalized, mechanized, and industrialized. These developments have produced large-scale, historically novel "ecotechnical" systems. These systems in turn operate as new environments within which natural selection operates. Food systems thus demonstrate how differences in scale produce emergent phenomena.

The first and most obvious aspect of this transformation is distance. While some food in the ancient period travelled significant distances, *most* food today is consumed a long way from its site of production. A 2002 Worldwatch Institute report noted that the average American food item travels between 1,500 and 2,500 miles from farm to plate (Halwell 2002). One oft-cited Swedish study from 1993 found that the components of a typical breakfast—apple, bread, cream, orange juice, sugar, and so on—travelled a distance approximating the earth's circumference before consumption (Pfeiffer 2006:25). This great expansion of the distances traversed by food was a consequence of the development of steam and internal combustion engines, meaning that today's food systems are heavily dependent upon fossil fuels. In contemporary America, 17 percent of all energy is used for the purposes of feeding, a figure divided roughly evenly between production, processing, and distribution/cooking (Nye 2006:82). The total energy cost of food thus significantly exceeds that of its production (Smil 2006:52).

The high-energy food economy allowed foodstuffs to move around the planet at historically unprecedented speeds. In the nineteenth century, for example, railroads and steamboats allowed the transportation of live animals across North America or the Atlantic Ocean. Time, contemporaries were fond of saying, was annihilating space. Cattle traveling on such ships would not have agreed: the journey was long and difficult, with illness and injury often decimating herds en route: in 1886, 5,907 animals had to be thrown overboard during Atlantic crossings (Bear 1888:93). Meanwhile, these systems efficiently distributed unwanted diseases like rinderpest and foot-and-mouth disease across greater distances, leading to a wave of European epizootics and emergency public health strategies ranging from culling to trade embargoes.

Transporting dead meat was promoted as more safe, efficient, and humane, but this raised the question of decay. The ultimate solution, mechanical refrigeration, was fully functional by the 1880s and was soon being used for the transportation and storage of meat, milk, and fruit through a "cold chain" that wove abattoirs, dairies, trains, storage depots, and delivery trucks into a relatively streamlined network characterized by calculated temperature control. The cold chain arrested decay and made foods more durable. Durability was also increasingly engineered into foodstuffs themselves through the use of preservatives, pasteurization, wrapping, and other techniques.

The emerging spatial pattern thus involved extremely elongated transportation and distribution chains linking large hubs where foodstuffs were stockpiled and processed. Grain elevators, mills, bakeries, sugar refineries, dairies, cold stores, feedlots, and abattoirs replaced smaller institutions and were often clustered in particular geographical zones (ports, urban peripheries). This substantial scaling-up of production involved new forms of construction, manipulation, and mechanization. Milling, baking, and refining, for example, became complex technological processes. Such economies of scale facilitated the accumulation of waste materials in sufficient quantities to make possible the profitable reuse of very small, biologically distinct parts of animals: abattoirs harvested glands for the pharmaceutical industry, for example.

Contemporary food systems have a number of defining characteristics. They consist of critical nodes linked by very long transportation and distribution chains. There is a quite substantial amount of slack between component parts; for example, between abattoir and fast food restaurant. This means that food disasters emerge slowly, unspectacularly, and insidiously, unlike, say, meltdowns in nuclear reactors or explosions in petrochemical plants (Perrow 1984). Moreover, despite the best efforts of those building them, food systems are never fully insulated from their environments: they are "ecotechnical," blurring the boundaries between "technology" and "nature." Their size, shape, and complexity necessitated governmental strategies such as inspection, but they remained impossible to fully predict and police. A working definition of complex modern food systems would include the significant distance between component parts and their openness, sprawling extent, and nodality: they are slack, slow, porous, opaque, and vulnerable (Hughes 1983). The food system itself is a metasystem composed of multiple, interlaced subsystems. For example, the Danish bacon industry grew up symbiotically with the dairying system: skimmed milk left over from making butter was fed to pigs.

The scaling-up of food systems thus produced historically novel ecologies: distended chains of controlled cold, for example, or the industrial slaughter of mass agglomerations of mammals. As complexity theorists have noted, when a system increases in scale, it frequently displays *emergent* properties. Emergence refers to the capacity of systems to generate genuinely novel phenomena: they are surprising. I conclude by examining one such emergent property of food systems: their tendency to create the ecological conditions of emergence and distribution of new forms of pathogen.

Viewed from the perspective of the microbiome, food systems were novel forms of evolutionary space. They provided new physical environments within which natural selection operated. Across food systems, strange new forms of life appeared: molds and slimes clinging tenaciously to the surfaces of frozen carcasses, or wingless insects devouring wheat in granaries. In the 1880s,

western European public health officials began to observe an increasing incidence of various types of food poisoning. These cases, they realized, were related to the physical conditions produced within modern food systems. Modern food poisoning was a consequence of extended food chains, their ecologies, and the food habits they engendered: prepared foods were more frequently cooked, cooled, and reheated, which gave pathogens opportunities to slowly multiply. Meat products and canned meats were particularly dangerous, especially foods like pork pies, whose jelly was an "admirable nutrient media for bacteria," particularly when slowly cooled (Savage 1920:168). Food handlers often displayed inadequate hygiene, not least because of poor sanitary facilities.

This process involved the effective distribution of previously unknown pathogens and, in some cases, the actual emergence of entirely new microbes that crossed species barriers as a result of the form of food systems. Salmonella was first identified in 1888: by 1962, 700 serotypes had been identified (Taylor 1962:15). Listeria was first recognized in 1929, and *Escherichia coli* O157: H7 was first recorded in 1982: the emergence and circulation of both appear to have been the result of intensive, industrial food production, particularly the development of the meat industry (Armstrong et al. 1996; Ojeniyi et al. 2000:306; Pennington 2003:96). In the same year, the term *prion* was first used to refer to numerous similar, but novel, disease agents apparently causing several mysterious brain diseases in humans and animals, including bovine spongiform encephalopathy (BSE) and Creutzfeldt-Jakob Disease (CJD) in humans. BSE had afflicted more than 36,000 cattle by 1992, and the British government responded by culling more than 100,000 cattle. BSE was an unpredictable consequence of decades of feeding cattle with meat and bonemeal recovered from abattoir waste. This practice can be dated back to late nineteenth-century meat complexes in South America, where cattle were described as being initially "reluctant" to eat it (Siderius 1893:30 cited in Schwartz 2003:146–47). Vague concerns were raised about the practice, but the assumption was that heat treatment would sterilize any disease agents (Moulton 1929:310). Unfortunately, and unpredictably, this new disease agent proved highly resistant both to heat and chemical disinfectants.

FOOD SYSTEMS CAN BEST BE CONCEPTUALIZED as giant "ecotechnologies" which extract, process, and distribute vast amounts of edible matter to human populations. They have generated unprecedented abundance for most inhabitants of the global north. Like all giant systems, however, they have also produced many unintended consequences, such as the globalization of epizootics, or the genetic homogenization of foodstuffs. One particularly important unintended consequence of large-scale food systems is the production and circulation of new and deadly pathogens. Food systems have thus generated, evolutionarily, novel foodborne risks that have produced reactive mitigation strategies ranging from Pulsenet, the American network that coordinates the molecular subtyping of foodborne pathogens, to mass cattle culls such as those seen in Britain following the BSE crisis. These heterogeneous strategies—some sophisticated, some brutal—illustrate the impossibility of fully governing large-scale food systems, an impossibility ultimately rooted in the fertile agency of life itself. ■

CHRIS OTTER *is Associate Professor of History at the Ohio State University.*

REFERENCES

Armstrong, Gregory L., Jill Hollingsworth, and J. Glenn Morris, Jr. 1996. "Emerging Foodborne Pathogens: Escherichia coli O157:H7 as a Model of Entry of a New Pathogen into the Food Supply of the Developed World." Epidemiologic Reviews 18(1):29-51.

Bear, William E. 1888. The British Farmer and His Competitors. London: Cassell & Company.

Capra, Fritjof. 2005. "Complexity and Life." Theory, Culture and Society 22(5):33-44.

Halweil, Brian. 2002. Home Grown: The Case For Local Food In A Global Market. Washington, DC: Worldwatch Institute.

Hughes, Thomas. 1983. Networks of Power: Electrification in Western Society. Baltimore: Johns Hopkins University Press.

Moulton, C. Robert. 1929. Meat Through the Microscope: Applications of Chemistry and the Biological Sciences to Some Problems of the Meat Packing Industry. Chicago, IL: University of Chicago Press.

Nye, David. 2006. Technology Matters: Questions to Live With. Cambridge, MA: MIT Press.

Ojeniyi, B., J. Christensen, and M. Bisgaard. 2000. "Comparative Investigations of Listeria monocytogenes Isolated from a Turkey Plant, Turkey Products, and from Human Cases of Listeriosis in Denmark." Epidemiology and Infection 125(2):303-308

Pennington, T. Hugh. 2003. When Food Kills: BSE, E Coli, and Disaster Science. Oxford, UK: Oxford University Press.

Perrow, Charles. 1984. Normal Accidents: Living with High-Risk Technologies. New York: Basic Books.

Pfeiffer, Dale Allen. 2006. Eating Fossil Fuels: Oil, Food and the Coming Crisis in Agriculture. Gabriola Island, BC, Canada: New Society Books.

Savage, William G. 1920. Food Poisoning and Food Infections. Cambridge, UK: Cambridge University Press.

Schwartz, Maxime. 2003. How the Cows Turned Mad. Berkeley: University of California Press.

Siderius, C. 1893. L'Alimentation des animaux domestiques, formulaires de rations. Paris: Ballière.

Smil, Vaclav. 2006. Energy: A Beginner's Guide. Oxford, UK: Oneworld.

Taylor, Joan. 1962. "Salmonella and Salmonellosis." In Food Poisoning: Symposium, edited by W. Charles Cockburn, Joan Taylor, E.S. Anderson, and Betty C. Hobbs, p. 15-32. London: The Royal Society of Health.

SCALING UP

SCALING DOWN

Sophie Dubuisson-Quellier shows how French markets and social movements interact in food provisioning.

LIKE EVERY THURSDAY AFTERNOON, CELINE'S TWO KIDS ARE exited, because Thursday is the *jour du Panier* ("basket day"). At 6 p.m., Celine and her two children meet other *amapiens* to receive their weekly basket of vegetables from La Ferme du Soleil. Pierre, the farmer from La Ferme du Soleil, is perfectly on time as he is every week, despite the fact that his farm is 15 kilometers from downtown. He unloads his cases of zucchini, lettuce, eggplant, cucumbers, and tomatoes, while Marc, who is in charge this month of the distribution, starts to count and weight the production to calculate how much of each vegetable each member of the Association pour le Maintien d'une Agriculture Paysanne (AMAP; similar to community-supported agriculture groups [CSAs] in the United States) will receive in his/her basket. Once he writes the contents of each basket on a sheet of cardboard, Cecile' kids start their favorite activity: taking from Pierre's cases the vegetables. This week it is three heads of lettuce, three eggplants, two kilos of tomatoes, two cucumbers...and three more kilos of zucchinis, a good occasion for them to tease their mother. This is the peak of the zucchini season, and Cecile really starts to get short on ideas for how to cook these vegetables. This became a subject of joke between the *amapiens* of La Ferme du Soleil, who exchange recipes to cope with the bumper crop!

Since the turn of the twentieth century, numerous new food provisioning systems have mushroomed in various Western countries, including fair trade, organic co-ops, small-scale farming, grass-fed meat, direct selling, cow share contracts, CSAS/AMAPS, and local food on restaurant menus (Dubuisson-Quellier 2013a). These initiatives receive extensive media coverage because most originate from a critical perspective fueled by anti-mass-consumption movements such as the antiglobalist, environmental, or social justice movements. They are generally presented in opposition to industrial food systems. But I would argue that the industrial and alternative systems in fact support each other.

Alternative food movements blame industrial agro-food systems for social injustices such as impoverishing small producers and for environmental damage such as polluting soil and decreasing biodiversity, as well as for cultural effects such as the homogenization of tastes and products. The issue of scale is at the core of these social critiques. According to the claims of these social movements, agro-food systems are organized through huge businesses. Long supply chains from farms to retailers that rely on specialization and concentration benefit from the effects of these large scales. As a consequence, consumers ignore or cannot see the social, economic, and environmental damage that these food systems cause. For the promoters of alternatives, scaling food systems down increases consumer awareness and reduces pressure on producers and the environment.

These alternative food systems shorten the geographical and organizational distance between producers and consumers. For example, fair trade operators draw small producers from the south to the attention of consumers from the north through diverse communication devices. Although the physical distances between the two types of actors remains large, the nongovernmental organizations

PHOTO BY MERLE JA JOONAS

(NGOs) involved in fair trade try to create a solidarity that is supposed to shorten these distances. In the case of CSAs, the idea is also to bridge consumption and production by organizing contractual systems between farmers and purchasers, who receive weekly baskets of fruits and vegetables that they have paid for before the start of the harvest season. The contract is supposed to organize solidarity between upstream and downstream actors in the supply chain, making the consumers more aware of farmers' risks and exigencies. Farmers' markets or local and organic co-ops also depend on proximity and small family farming. They posit that not only should distance be decreased, but also that the scale of production should be downsized. Across all these alternative food systems, small-scale becomes a motto and an approach in opposition to huge globalized food systems (Weber et al. 2008).

This polarized vision might have some rhetorical virtues for those who promote alternative food systems, but both systems are in fact intertwined, giving life to a moving process through which food systems are constantly evolving, regenerating, and—most important—internalizing the social critiques they face.

Therefore, it might be more appropriate to analyze scaling as a process rather than considering scales as fixed and rigid features of food systems.

Let's take, for example, what is happening in France around the phenomenon of alternative food systems. Neither producers nor consumers evolve in a closed world of either large-scale or small-scale food systems. Most consumers who are members of an AMAP do not stop shopping from big retail companies. They usually use have diverse provisioning strategies. And producers have multiple retailing strategies; although most specialize by selling only through an AMAP, a few of them also adopt other direct-selling strategies through a producer shop, a farmer's market, or online delivery. Moreover, some farmers who sell directly from the farm may continue to work with big producer organizations, retailers, and wholesalers. Thus, in these two supposedly separate worlds—one for small farmers directly selling to activist consumers, and the other with big farms and retailers selling to mass consumers—actors in fact allocate their choices in a plurality of ways, composing heterogeneous food systems.

The price setting within most AMAPs

is also illuminating. The code of conduct that is supposed to rule the different local contracts says that the price of farm shares should reflect farmers' production costs to oppose and contest the tendency of globalized food systems to lower prices to capture mass consumption. The AMAP system intends to help farmers live decently from their work by setting prices that cover their real costs. But, in fact, it is very difficult for a small farm to calculate their production costs for each of its products. Doing so would require farmers to calculate the time they allocate for each of their interventions on each crop: seeding, monitoring, watering, harvesting, etc. In small-scale farms, where a single farmer does everything, this can be known only very approximately. And even though some farmers would be able to calculate it (thanks to a profound passion for cost accounting!), the cost would not mechanically set the price. In fact, like most other economic actors, most AMAP farmers set prices according to those of their nearby competitors. They use prices from supermarkets, organic co-ops, other AMAPs, or farmers' markets to decide the prices of their basket. As one farmer told me, "Well, I do not want to compete too much with the co-op that offered to deliver my baskets in front of its shop!" AMAPs are not out of the market but part of it, interacting with other food systems. As a consequence, alternative food systems should not be considered as operating in a separate world from other supply chains, but simply as part of a general food system.

One might argue that, yes, they are alternative and different because they operate on smaller scales. But actually, the scaling is a process rather than a feature, both because small and large operators interact and because these operators evolve. Some operators in alternative food systems are considering scaling up since they face a surfeit of success among consumers. For example, most of the AMAPs have waiting lists of consumers who want to be members but cannot enter since the farmer cannot (or does not want to) produce more. Even though each group should not exceed a certain number of families (40 is common), some groups have become even larger. Indeed, the demand substantially exceeds the supply; because farmers are lacking, some of them expand or associate with others to deliver to larger groups of consumers. These increases in scale create debates within the AMAP communities.

Within the fair trade world, scaling up became a big issue at the beginning of the twenty-first century with two of the main historical operators in France. While Artisans du Monde, one of the oldest fair trade NGOs, refused to contract with big retailing companies, the Max Havelaar association decided scaling up was the only suitable way to reach more consumers, arguing that doing so could ultimately convince supermarkets to change their practices. In reality, this debate about scale hid a more profound opposition between the different business models and conceptions of the role of consumers in these alternative food systems. Since Max Havelaar earns money from the royalties it receives from the brand that uses its labels on their packaging, it is trying to reach a greater amount of consumers, even if they are only occasional consumers of fair trade products. But Artisans du Monde earns money from its own retailing and wholesaling activities. It considers sales of fair trade products as a means rather than an end, to reach consumers and deliver complete information about social justice issues. As a consequence, scaling up was not as important as making sure that consumers become proselytes of the cause. Thus, what is at stake in questions of scale in alternative food systems is in fact the nature of the collective action in each alternative food system as well as the economic considerations they face as market operators.

At the same time, one has also to understand that operators who are traditionally associated with the globalized industrial agro-food system are beginning to see alternative food systems as business opportunities. In France as in other countries, supermarkets and manufacturers may have at first ignored fair trade, local food, direct selling, and other alternative systems as piteous competitors. But they progressively changed their minds. In the food sector, where markets are largely saturated, fair trade, organic products, and local food have become new and profitable market niches. Many manufacturers have developed organic, fair-trade products or "made in France" products, while retailers have developed local supplies. Sourcing activities thus increasingly merge large-scale and small-scale systems.

Of course, this fine intertwinement between different scales produces frictions in markets and in social movements. Resource partitioning theory posits that markets may be separated between a few dominant large-scale and highly concentrated generalist companies on one side and, on the other, small-scale entrepreneurs supported by identity movements and nourished by anti-mass-production sentiment that resists homogenization. This is the case for microbreweries (Carroll and Swaminathan 2000), independent bookselling (Miller 2006), and alternative media (Greeve et al. 2006). But such partitions can in fact be rather blurred when small-scale operations cease to be constitutive of identities. This is increasingly the case in the organic food industry, in which operators can be both small and large (Sikavica and Pozner 2013). This phenomenon accounts directly for the capacity of social movement organizations to operate as real market actors (Dubuisson-Quellier 2013b; Lounsbury et al. 2003), and of the market to endogenize their critics (Boltanski and Chiapello 1999). Both of these mechanisms are part of the dynamics of food systems. ∎

SOPHIE DUBUISSON-QUELLIER is *research professor at Sciences Po and works at the Centre de sociologie des organisations, in Paris. She works in economic sociology and on the interactions between firms, markets and social movements.*

REFERENCES

Boltanski L., and E. Chiapello. 2005. *The New Spirit of Capitalism.* London-New York, Verso.

Carroll G., and A. Swaminathan. 2000. "Why the Microbrewery Movement? Organizational Dynamics of Resource Partitioning in the U.S. Brewing Industry." *American Journal of Sociology* 106(3):715–62.

Dubuisson-Quellier S. 2013a. Ethical Consumption. Toronto, Canada: Fernwood Publishing.

———. 2013b. "A Market Mediation Strategy: How Social Movements Seek To Change Firms' Practices by Promoting New Principles of Product Valuation." *Organization Studies* 34(5–6):683–703.

Greeve H. R., J.-E. Pozner, and H. Rao. 2006. "Vox Populi: Resource Partitioning, Organizational Proliferation, and the Cultural Impact of the Insurgent Microradio Movement." *American Journal of Sociology* 112:802–37.

Lounsbury M., M. Ventresca, and P. Hirsch. 2003. "Social Movements, Field Frames and Industry Emergence: A Cultural-Political Perspective on U.S. Recycling." *Socio-Economic Review* 1:71–104.

Miller L. 2006. *Reluctant Capitalists: Bookselling and the Culture of Consumption.* Chicago, IL: University of Chicago Press

Sikavica K., and J.-E. Pozner. 2013. "Paradise Sold: Resource Partitioning Theory and the Organic Movement in the US Farming Industry." *Organization Studies* 34(5–6):623–51.

Weber K., K. Heinze, and M. DeSoucey. 2008. "Forage for Thought: Mobilizing Codes in the Movement for Grass-Fed Meat and Dairy Products." *Administrative Science Quarterly* 53:529–67.

The Silence of the Labs

Is sugar a choice? **Kim Hendrickx** explores how a Sugar Museum in Belgium puts life and health into perspective.

A SWEET LANDSCAPE

Haspengouw is a region in Belgium known for its fertile soil, fruit orchards, and fields cultivated with wheat and sugar beet. It is arguably the country's sweetest region. But if the region's apple and pear orchards stand for healthy sweetness, then what does the sugar beet and its refined sugar stand for today? Sugar has become suspect since the late 1970s (Brody 1977), and the debate on sugar's responsibility for chronic ailments such as diabetes and obesity continues today.[1] "Sugar is 'addictive and the most dangerous drug of the times,'" says a recent *Telegraph* headline (Waterfield 2013).[2] For the municipality of Tienen, home of the biggest sugar refinery in Belgium, sugar is entwined with local history.[3] The factory brought industrial development to a nineteenth-century agrarian community, employment, local festivals with fireworks in the early twentieth century, and a rock festival today called *Suikerrock* (Sugar Rock). In 2002, the municipality opened a museum devoted to sugar. The relation of the factory to community life is evoked through different aspects: labor and harvesting techniques, sugar beet types, local political personalities, and historical events. Two exhibition rooms, however, cut the threads with community life and establish a different connection between sugar and humans. What's going on here?

THE SILENT LABORATORY

"Silence, dear visitor, only silence is appropriate here. We have entered the sanctuary of the sugar factory...the laboratory!"

Thus goes the voice of Professor Zucchero, our audioguide. It is interesting that the guide should be a scientist. He is a typical nutty professor who has privileged access to what sugar and sweetness are all about: a molecular connection. The eye-catcher in the room is a giant microscope: a *macroscope*. It certainly catches the visitor's eye, and the play of scales transforms the visitor *into* an eye, turning his/her entire body into a witness of the molecular miracle of sugar, the *tango d'amore* between glucose and fructose. The visitor is allowed to witness the spectacle in respectful silence. It is not entirely clear what sort of laboratory this is. The only things on display are different types of sugar, more or less refined. There are also some antique measuring devices. An explanation is provided about inulin as well, a sugar replacer with health benefits for your intestinal flora, developed by a spin-off of the sugar refinery in the 1990s. So it would seem that research is carried out here as well. But why are we asked to keep quiet in the laboratory? Isn't this the place where instruments are adjusted and cursed upon, results discussed, and questions raised? Where are all the people? We see none of Zucherro's colleagues at work, but only mute objects that relate to sugar in its different molecular and macroscopic forms.

THE ROOM OF STATEMENTS

"Opinions on the effects of sugar on health vary widely.... [W]e hope that you, as the judge, will make a reasonable stand for sugar."

The quote comes from an information board, the first of a series of boards that present scientific controversies on sugar as court cases. For each case, there is an imagined attorney general accusing sugar of being bad for one or

---

1   "Is Sugar Toxic?" asks Gary Taubes in the *New York Times* (2011), while referring to the scientific work of Robert Lustig on the relation between sugar and chronic ailments such as obesity and diabetes. See also Perreti (2012).
2   The title quotes Dutch health official Paul van der Velpen.
3   The refinery is now part of the German Group Südzucker, the EU's largest sugar producer.

other aspect of health. Next, the "sugar lawyer" responds by putting things in perspective. For the final verdict, the visitor's speech is restored but in a very specific mode: that of a judge.

After being reconfigured to a witnessing organ of perception in the laboratory, the visitor is now rescaled to his normal everyday bodily proportions, and a shift is made from the ability to perceive to the *competence* to judge.[4] He is no longer in the secluded space of the lab but in what seems to be a public space, where all sorts of rumors, opinions, data, and eating habits abound. He is asked to balance and judge. A visual cue, however, sharing the room with the courtroom cases, is proposed to help the visitor with this difficult task. In a corner easily visible from all points of view, we see two real and full-sized *exercise bicycles*.

How is it that *exercise bicycles* can be incorporated in a museum devoted to *sugar*? The simple answer is that the museum wants to convey the message that physical exercise is as important to health as the food we eat. Sugar itself cannot be responsible for obesity or diabetes. Things must be "put in perspective" if we want to judge the health risks of sugar properly. And for the visitor to judge properly, the museum uses interesting techniques of creating such contexts.

JUDGING PROPERLY

Putting things in perspective or "in their context" is not about simply standing back and looking at the bigger picture. On the contrary, it is a technical gesture. Think about statistics, for example, or the choices a curator is confronted with when designing an exhibition (for example, see MacDonald 1996). These two exhibition rooms make a number of interesting moves in terms of scales and rhythm. First, there is the alternation between speaking and silence. This alternation occurs not only between spaces—the lab or public space—but also between concerns. The concern in the laboratory is the delicate process of sucrose production. Silencing the visitor means rescaling him to the size of a microscope and folding him up so that only his eye remains. Historians and philosophers of science argue that experimental apparatuses not only produce data or "matters of fact," but also shut the mouths of critics (Stengers 1999).

The history of experimental science shows that knowledge and social order were intimately linked: who can talk when and where, and pose legitimate problems (Shapin and Schaffer 1985)? The sugar museum also has its way of distributing speech and silence, and framing legitimate problems. The lab of the sugar factory is more than a laboratory: it is a sanctuary. We can watch, but not meddle in sacred affairs: the play of scales and silence allow objects to articulate a behavioral code that connects knowledge and social order.

By contrast, in the second room, all sorts of opinions abound. Statements about the health effects of sugar are presented as legitimate concerns, albeit for *private consideration*. The visitor is invited to make a *private* and singularized judgement in public space. It is through the individual that things can be "put in perspective." Next to the plays of silence and speech, and the play of scales between sugar molecules and the visitor's body, the exercise bicycles are part of the museum's technique to put things in perspective and to show how one must judge properly. Is sugar bad for my health? It depends. Do I exercise enough? By privatizing these questions, the museum bypasses the formulation of collective concerns about sugar and health. It is up to individuals/visitors to make up their own minds about health and healthy living (see MacDonald 1996).

SUGAR AND SOCIAL LIFE

The paradox of this story is that nearly all exhibition rooms celebrate sugar as a collective phenomenon. The visitor appreciates how sugar changed the face of a once-agrarian town and established a network of dispersed refineries, sugar beet cultivations, and a flux of beets and

---

4   I want to suggest that individuals' critical competencies, enabling them to judge, are hijacked, deformed, and put on stage again through the figure of the "consumer." Likewise, in neo-management practice, a version of the notion of "competence" is mobilized that takes advantage of the vagueness with regards to its requirements, in contrast to officially agreed-upon qualifications. See Boltanski and Chiapello (2005), for example.

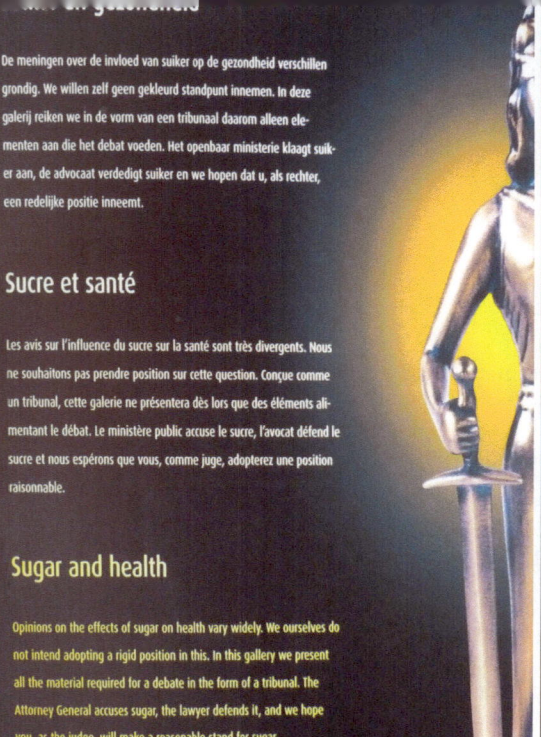

Exercise Bikes in the Museum **LEFT:** Sugar, Health, and Lady Justice (PHOTOS BY ARTICLE AUTHOR)

workers within a broader geographic region. Sugar has tied people together through local festivities, right up to today's Sugar Rock festival, which is sponsored by the factory. But as soon as we approach sugar *itself*, strange things happen. Our social ties with sugar are cut. First of all, sugar becomes a matter of *science*: not just chemistry, but *sacred* chemistry that we should not meddle with. Second, when we touch upon the question of sugar's health risks, our sweet molecule is not allowed to partake in social life either. When asked to make a judgement in front of an exercise bike, one may wonder what happened to all the human, technical, and political resources necessary to make sugar's existence possible and virtually omnipresent in packaged food products.

To conclude, I must admit that I have grown fond of this particular sugar museum because it superbly succeeds in articulating a political difference between sugar as a sociotechnical *accomplishment* and sugar as an individual *choice*. The naturalness and logic of having production "on the one hand" and consumption "on the other" becomes wonderfully complicated and visible through the museum's techniques of display. ■

KIM HENDRICKX *is an anthropologist at the Spiral Research Centre (University of Liège, Belgium), and he is currently finalizing a PhD about food-related health claims.*

REFERENCES

Boltanski, L., and E. Chiapello. 2005. *The New Spirit of Capitalism.* London: Verso.

Brody, Jane E. 1977. "Villain in Disguise?" *New York Times*, May 25, p. 53.

MacDonald, S. 1996. "Authorising Science: Public Understanding of Science in Museums." In *Misunderstanding Science? The Public Reconstruction of Science and Technology*, edited by A. Irwin and B. Wynne, 152–71. Cambridge, UK: Cambridge University Press.

Perreti, Jacques. 2012. "What Caused the Obesity Crisis in the West?" *BBC News*, June 13. http://www.bbc.co.uk/news/health-18393391.

Shapin, S., and S. Schaffer. 1985 *Leviathan and the Air-Pump: Hobbes, Boyle, and the Experimental Life.* Princeton, NJ: Princeton University Press.

Stengers, I. 1999. *L'Invention des Sciences Modernes.* Paris: Flammarion.

Taubes, Gary. 2011. "Is Sugar Toxic?" *New York Times*, April 13. http://www.nytimes.com/2011/04/17/magazine/mag-17Sugar-t.html?pagewanted=all&_r=0.

Westfield, Bruno. 2013. "Sugar Is 'Addictive and The Most Dangerous Drug of the Times.'" *Telegraph*, September 17. http://www.telegraph.co.uk/news/worldnews/europe/netherlands/10314705/Sugar-is-addictive-and-the-most-dangerous-drug-of-the-times.html.

MENHADEN [Brevoortia tyrannus]

David Schleifer and **Alison Fairbrother** introduce Menhaden, the fish you've never heard of but are probably eating right now.

THE FISH AT THE HEART OF THE FOOD SYSTEM

You have never seen a menhaden, but you have eaten one. Although no one sits down to a plate of these silvery, bug-eyed, foot-long fish at a seafood restaurant, menhaden travel through the human food chain mostly undetected in the bodies of other species, hidden in salmon, pork, onions, and many other foods.

Millions of pounds of menhaden are fished from the Atlantic Ocean and the Gulf of Mexico by a single company based in Houston, Texas, with a benign-sounding name: Omega Protein. The company's profits derive largely from a process called "reduction," which involves cooking, grinding, and chemically separating menhaden's fat from its protein and micronutrients. These component parts become chemical inputs in aquaculture, industrial livestock, and vegetable growing. The oil- and protein-rich meal becomes animal feed. The micronutrients become crop fertilizer.

It works like this: from April to December, the tiny coastal town of Reedville, Virginia, sends dozens of fishermen into the Chesapeake Bay and the Atlantic Ocean on Omega Protein's nine ships. Spotter pilots in small aircraft fly overhead, looking for menhaden from above, which are recognizable by the reddish shadow they leave on the water as they pack together in tight schools of tens of thousands of fish.

When menhaden are identified, the spotter pilots radio to the nearest ship and direct it to the school. Omega Protein's fishermen dispatch two smaller boats, which trap the school with a giant net

called a purse seine. When the fish are enclosed, the purse seine net is cinched tight like a drawstring. A hydraulic vacuum pump then sucks the menhaden from the net into the hold of the ship. Back at the factory, reduction begins. A similar process occurs in the Gulf of Mexico, where Omega Protein owns three reduction factories.

MORE MENHADEN ARE CAUGHT than any other fish in the continental United States by volume. Until recently, this massive operation and its products were almost entirely unregulated, despite a substantial ecological impact. The menhaden population has declined nearly 90 percent from the time when humans first began harvesting menhaden from Atlantic coastal and estuarine waters.

Omega Protein was hardly the first to recognize menhaden's value. The etymology of menhaden indicates its longstanding place in food production. Its name derives from the Narragansett word *munnawhatteaûg*, which literally means "that which enriches the land." Archeological research on Cape Cod shows that Native Americans there buried fish believed to be menhaden in their cornfields (Mrozowski 1994:47–62). William Bradford and Edward Winslow's firsthand account from 1622 of the Pilgrims at Plymouth, Massachusetts, describes the colonists manuring their farm plots with fish "according to the manner of the Indians" (Bradford and Winslow 1622).

Entrepreneurs as early as the eighteenth century began to build small

facilities to reduce menhaden into oil and meal for use in industrial and agricultural products. By the mid-twentieth century, more than two hundred of these facilities dotted the east coast of the United States and the Gulf of Mexico. For most of those years, fishermen caught menhaden using nets they hauled in by hand. But starting in the 1950s, hydraulic vacuum pumps made it possible to suck millions of menhaden from larger nets into giant tanker ships. In the past 60 years, 47 billion pounds of menhaden have been harvested from the Atlantic.

As the menhaden catch grew, small factories and fishing fleets went out of business. By 2006, only one company was left standing. Omega Protein, headquartered in Texas, catches between a quarter and a half-billion pounds of menhaden each year from the Atlantic, and nearly double that amount from the Gulf of Mexico.

Because Omega Protein dominates the industry, its annual investor reports make it possible to trace menhaden through the global food chain from its reduction facility in Reedville, Virginia, and handful of factories in Louisiana and Mississippi.

CONSISTENT WITH NATIVE AMERICAN usage, menhaden micronutrients—principally nitrogen, phosphorus, and potassium—are used to make fertilizers. In the United States, menhaden-based fertilizers are used to grow onions in Texas, blueberries in Georgia, and roses in Tennessee, among other crops.

A small portion of the fats are used to

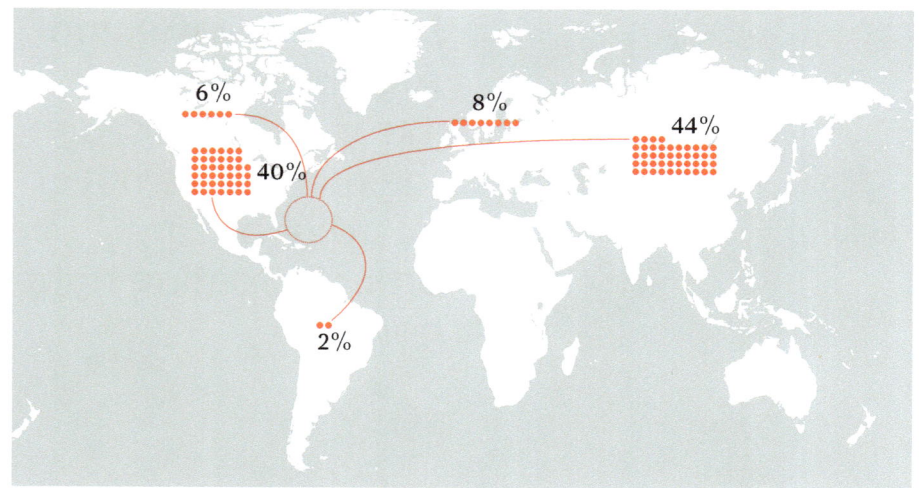

GLOBAL MENHADEN SALES: Omega Protein harvests nearly a quarter billion menhaden from Virginia waters. Just 40% of Omega Protein's revenue comes from the U.S. sales. Most menhaden end up abroad.
SOURCE: OMEGA PROTEIN, MAY 2013
"THE U.S. OMEGA 3 AND OMEGA 6 MARKETS."

make human nutritional supplements, namely fish oil pills containing omega-3 fatty acids, which have been associated with a reduction in some risk factors for heart disease. Omega-3s are found naturally in some green vegetables and nuts. They're also in algae, which menhaden consume in large quantities. As a result, menhaden and the fish species that rely on menhaden for food are full of omega-3s.

In 2004, the US Food and Drug Administration allowed manufacturers to make claims on food packages linking consumption of foods containing omega-3s to a reduced risk of heart disease. Whether or not taking omega-3 fish oil pills has the same benefits as eating foods that contain omega-3s remains a matter of debate (Allport 2006; Kris-Etherton et al. 2002; Rizos et al. 2012). Nonetheless, sales of fish oil pills grew from $100 million in 2001 to $1.1 billion in 2011 (Frost & Sullivan Research Service 2008; Herper 2009; Packaged Facts 2011). The market for omega-3 supplements and for foods and beverages fortified with omega-3s was $195 million in 2004. By 2011, it was estimated at $13 billion.

For Omega Protein, the real money is in menhaden proteins and fats, which have become ingredients in animal feed for industrial-scale aquaculture, swine, and cattle growing operations in the United States and abroad. The company is well positioned to continue expanding sales of menhaden around the world. While the global supply of both fats and proteins have been flat since 2004, demand has grown considerably. Omega Protein's revenue per ton has more than tripled since 2000. Total revenues were $236 million in 2012, a 17.8 percent gross margin.

OMEGA PROTEIN'S "BLUE CHIP" customer base for animal feed and human supplements includes Whole Foods, Nestlé Purina, Iams, Land O'Lakes, ADM, Swanson Health Products, Cargill, Del Monte, Science Diet, Smart Balance, and the Vitamin Shoppe. But the companies that buy menhaden meal and oil from Omega Protein are not required to label whether their products contain the fish, making it impossible for consumers to identify whether they are ingesting menhaden. However, given the volume of the fishery and the scale of Omega Protein's distribution, if you have sautéed farm-raised salmon or rendered supermarket bacon, you have likely eaten animals raised at least in part on menhaden. You may have also fed animals raised on menhaden to your pets, swallowed menhaden in gel capsules recommended by your cardiologist, or sprinkled them on your backyard vegetable garden.

"We've evolved the company over time to where you can get up in the morning, have an Omega-3 (fish oil) supplement to start your day, you can curb your hunger between meals with a protein shake, and you can sit down at dinner with a piece of salmon, and chances are, one of our products was used to help raise that salmon," Omega Protein CEO Brett Scholtes said in a recent interview with the *Houston Business Journal* (Ryan 2013).

WHY DOES IT MATTER THAT THIS tiny fish is used to fuel the growing global demand for animal protein as global incomes rise and diets change (WHO 2013:5)? Because menhaden are not only valuable to the human food supply, they are also linchpins of the oceanic food chain.

Menhaden spawn in the ocean, but most of the fish head to the Chesapeake Bay to grow older in the brackish waters of the nation's largest estuary. Historically, the Chesapeake Bay supported a huge population of menhaden: legend has it that Captain John Smith saw so many menhaden packed into Chesapeake Bay when he arrived in 1607 that he could catch them with a frying pan.

In this nursery environment, menhaden grow and thrive in large schools before migrating up and down the Atlantic coast. These menhaden schools supply vital, nutritious food for dozens of important predators, like striped bass, weakfish, bluefish, spiny dogfish, dolphins, humpback whales, harbor seals, osprey, loons, and more.

In 2009, fisheries scientists reported that the Atlantic menhaden population had shrunk to less than 10 percent of its original size. Industry scientists argue that little prey fish like menhaden, sardines, and herring reproduce fast enough to replace those that are removed from the ocean food chain by commercial fishing. But many environmentalists, government and academic scientists, and coastal residents argue that menhaden fishing destabilizes ecosystems, leaving too few menhaden in the water to account for predator demand.

Striped bass have long been one of the most voracious predators of menhaden on the East Coast. Today, many striped bass in the Chesapeake Bay are afflicted with mycobacteriosis, a previously rare lesion-causing disease linked to malnutrition.

Osprey, another menhaden predator,

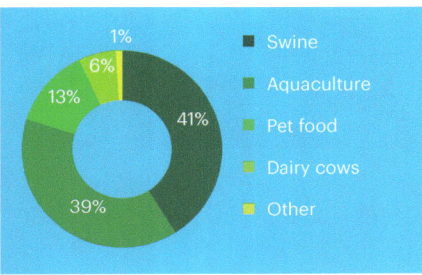

PROTEIN: 72% of Omega Protein's revenue comes from menhaden protein processed into animal feed.

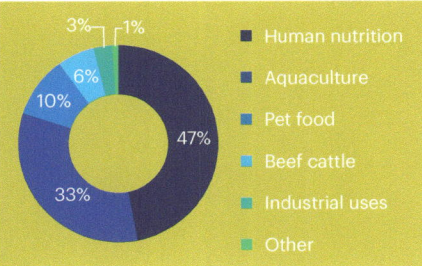

LIPIDS: 19% of Omega Protein's revenue comes from menhaden fats processed into animal feed and into omega-3 pills and IV drips for human nutrition.

MICRONUTRIENTS AND WHEY: 9% of Omega protein's revenue comes from menhaden micronutrients processed into fertilizer and from secondary business that processes whey protein from dairy into human nutritional supplements and food ingredients.

SOURCE: OMEGA PROTEIN, MAY 2013
"THE U.S. OMEGA 3 AND OMEGA 6 MARKETS"

have not fared much better. In the 1980s, more than 70 percent of the osprey diet was menhaden. By 2006, that number had fallen to 27 percent, and the survival of osprey nestlings in Virginia had fallen to its lowest levels since the 1940s, when the insecticide DDT was introduced to the area, which decimated the osprey young. And in the mid-2000s, researchers began finding that weakfish, an economically important predator fish in the Atlantic Ocean, were dying in high numbers. Without a healthy, plentiful stock of menhaden on which to feed, striped bass were preying on small weakfish and substantially reducing their population.

In 2012, a panel of marine experts known as the Lenfest Forage Fish Task Force estimated that the value of leaving forage fish in the ocean as a food source for predators was $11 billion: twice as much as the $5.6 billion generated by removing species like menhaden from the

ocean and pressing them into fish meal pellets (Pikitch et al, 2012).

After decades of advocacy by environmental organizations, in December 2012, a regulatory agency called the Atlantic States Marine Fisheries Commission implemented the first ever coast-wide regulation of the menhaden fishery. The Commission cut the menhaden harvest by 20 percent from previous levels in an attempt to safeguard the population from further decline. The regulation was implemented during the 2013 fishing season; whether it has affected the menhaden population is a question government scientists are scrambling to answer.

Meanwhile, menhaden products remain vital to global production of cheap fish and meat. The industrial food system relies on extracting nutrients from wild animal bodies. We consume menhaden in the form of pork chops, chicken breast, and tilapia. And in doing so, our eating habits lead to the deaths of birds and predator fish that never actually pass our lips. ■

ALISON FAIRBROTHER *is the executive director of the Public Trust Project, a nonpartisan, nonprofit organization that investigates and reports on misrepresentations of science by corporations, government, and the media.*

DAVID SCHLEIFER *researches and writes about food, healthcare, technology and education. He is also a senior research associate at Public Agenda, a nonpartisan, nonprofit research and engagement organization.*

The views expressed here are not necessarily those of Public Agenda or its funders.

REFERENCES

Allport, Susan. 2006. *The Queen of Fats: Why Omega-3s Were Removed from the Western Diet and What We Can Do to Replace Them.* Berkeley CA: University of California Press.

Bradford, William, and Edward Winslow. 1622. *A Relation or Journall of the Beginning and Proceedings of the English Plantation Settled at Plimoth in New England, by Certaine English Adventurers Both Merchants and Others.* books.google.com/books?isbn=0918222842

Franklin, H. Bruce, 2007. *The Most Important Fish in the Sea: Menhaden and America.* Washington DC: Island Press.

Frost & Sullivan Research Service. 2008. "The U.S. Omega 3 and Omega 6 Markets." November 13. http://www.frost.com/prod/servlet/report-brochure.pag?id=N416-01-00-00-00.

Herper, Mathew. 2009. "One Supplement That Works." *Forbes,* August 20. http://www.forbes.com/forbes/2009/0907/executive-health-vitamins-science-supplements-omega-3.html.

Pikitch, Ellen, Dee Boersma, Ian Boyd, David Conover, Phillipe Curry, Tim Essington, Selina Heppell, Ed Houde, Marc Mangel, Daniel Pauly, Éva Plagányi, Keith Sainsbury, and Bob Steneck. 2012. "Little Fish, Big Impact: Managing a Crucial Link in Ocean Food Webs." Lenfest Ocean Program: Washington, DC.

Kris-Etherton, Penny M., William S. Harris, and Lawrence J. Appel. 2002. "Fish Consumption, Fish Oil, Omega-3 Fatty Acids, and Cardiovascular Disease." *Circulation* 106:2747–57.

Mrozowski, Stephen A. "The Discovery of a Native American Cornfield on Cape Cod." *Archaeology of Eastern North America* (1994): 47–62.

Packaged Facts. 2011. "Omega-3: Global Product Trends and Opportunities." September 1. http://www.packagedfacts.com/Omega-Global-Product-6385341/.

Rizos, E. C., E. E. Ntzani, E. Bika, M. S. Kostapanos, and M. S. Elisaf. 2012. "Association Between Omega-3 Fatty Acid Supplementation and Risk of Major Cardiovascular Disease Events: A Systematic Review and Meta-analysis." *Journal of the American Medical Association* 308(10):1024–33.

Ryan, Molly. 2013. "Omega Protein's CEO wants to help make you healthier." *Houston Business Journal,* September 27. http://www.bizjournals.com/houston/blog/nuts-and-bolts/2013/09/omega-proteins-ceo-wants-to-help-you.html

World Health Organization. 2013. "Global and Regional Food Consumption Patterns and Trends: Availability and Changes in Consumption of Animal Products." http://www.who.int/nutrition/topics/3_foodconsumption/en/index4.html.

TROJAN CANS

How did the self-service economy emerge? **Franck Cochoy** displays the 'pico-infrastructure' behind modern consumption.

CLASSIC BUSINESS HISTORY links the evolution of markets and consumption to underlying macro, classic, and web-like infrastructures such as energy grids, transportation systems, and communication networks, which have transformed the economy. However, recent scholarship has also addressed the impact of small, mundane, and "disconnected" market-things as market drivers. In this tradition, I look at "canned goods" (Hine, 1999; Strasser, 1989; Twede, 2012) as an underappreciated but highly important "pico-infrastructure" underlying these same transformations.

More precisely, cans were like an inverted Trojan horse, transforming American consumption just like the Greeks' gift to king Priam reversed the course of the Trojan War. In the myth, the spectacular free seductions of the container—the horse—served as a voluntary means to introduce a hidden content: a military squad with defined purposes. By contrast, with ordinary canned goods, the hidden paying promises of the content—the canned good—served as an involuntary way to introduce a visible container: the can. Despite its visibility, this container carried less-foreseeable implications. The can's ability to be read, stacked, and manipulated without affecting its content helped goods move beyond the limit of the counter, escape the retailers' mediation, and be handled directly by consumers. Well before the advent of supermarkets, cans thus heralded the shift from service to self-service arrangement, the rise of modern consumerism, and the development of the brand economy. The spread of canned goods after World War I triggered an unplanned shift of market infrastructures and structures: in advocating preserved foods and the technical means to carry them, their promoters more or less surreptitiously introduced important changes linked to the features of this new container.[1]

A CHANGE OVER TIME

Progressive Grocer, a trade journal founded in 1922 that targeted small, independent grocers and played a key role in promoting canned goods, advertised the can's two distinct advantages: the ability to transcend seasonality and the power to store foods. In its very first year of publication, the magazine launched a "Canned Foods Week" that became a yearly event each fall (October 1922: 7 sq.). Stressing—or rather constructing—the seasonality of cans, along the principle that "every business has its harvest period" (October 1924: 9), may seem totally paradoxical.[2] Indeed, aren't cans actually intended to transcend seasons, allowing the consumption of produce throughout the year? Yes, but *Progressive Grocer*'s marketing genius was to note that the natural seasonality of fresh produce can build the commercial seasonality of the containers aimed at preserving it. It is precisely when fresh produce becomes scarce—when the fall season comes (November 1923: 11)—that it becomes possible to sell the solutions that claim to compensate for such a shortage. *Progressive Grocer* invented the annual autumn can fair as a device designed to capture, along a sexist and almost animal scheme, the squirrel that supposedly hides inside each consumer:

> Even in this day of prompt delivery, women have a feeling of security if they have a well-filled cellar or pantry (November 1923: 11).

> [In the fall] [t]he old nesting instinct arises in the breast of the housewife and she wants to fill the larder (October 1924: 10).

The autumn moment and, more broadly, the 1920s, were indeed very favorable conditions for the consumption of canned food. Domestic refrigerators, introduced in the previous decade (Anderson, 1953), were still very rare. Therefore, most consumers continued to adapt, as they always did, to the seasonal eclipse of fresh produce. Traditionally, families prepared preserves for the winter, and the consumption of dried fruit and smoked meat was still part of American life. Thus, the burdens of the past created promising conditions for the development of a future market. Such a project was not totally obvious, of course: if the wide acceptance of substitutes for fresh food created a favorable environment for the consumption of canned foods, the habit of homemade preserves was a clear obstacle to their commercialization. But again, the general evolution of the economy and the American society changed the odds: *Progressive Grocer* noted that more than half the population lived in cities, away from the individual gardens that supported self-production, hence the likely decline in homemade preserves and the corresponding rise of a market for their industrial substitutes (October 1923: 23).

---

1. Of course, canned foods existed from the early nineteenth century, but the production of tins was industrialized from 1881 only and the totally hermetic modern tin (without the hole on the top of its ancestor) was invented in 1897 only. Based on these innovations, the commercial boom of canned foods begun only after World War I, with a shift in value from $100 million a year to more than $300 million between 1915 and 1920 (Twede, 1912).

2. All parenthetical citations for *Progressive Grocer* indicate the month and year of publication and page number(s).

Modern Merchandising

THE old-time store-keeper kept only what he knew people wanted to buy. The modern merchant makes people want to buy what he has to sell. That is modern merchandising.

Your own customers, Mr. Grocer, buy ten times as much milk from others as they buy from the grocer.

There are greater possibilities of increased business for the grocer on milk than on any other item you can sell.

More than half of your best customers are reading Pet Milk color pages in national magazines. On those pages we are telling your customers why they should buy their milk from

the grocer—telling why Pet Milk is the safest, most convenient and most economical form of milk for every household use.

Pet Milk displayed in your store and window reminds your customers of the story we have been telling them and advertising your advertising—tells them again in your store why they should buy their milk from the grocer.

When you display Pet Milk you appeal to people who are "almost persuaded." You tell them once more to buy their milk from the grocer—and you sell them.

That is modern merchandising.

PET MILK COMPANY
(Originators of evaporated milk) Arcade Bldg., St. Louis, Mo.

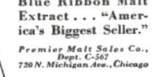

"The *Most Profitable Space in my Store* —

—is the space I use for Blue Ribbon Malt Extract."

"Every can of Blue Ribbon Malt represents so large a profit compared with the small space it takes up and it sells so fast that I've dropped slow-moving brands. From now on—it's Blue Ribbon for me!"
—So writes Jos. Sanguinetti, dealer of San Francisco.

A tip for you—friend dealer! Protect your shelf space. Stick to the brand that sells—and sells fast—Blue Ribbon Malt Extract . . . "America's Biggest Seller."

Premier Malt Sales Co.,
Dept. C-562
720 N. Michigan Ave., Chicago

Blue Ribbon Malt Extract
America's Biggest Seller
and getting Bigger every Day!

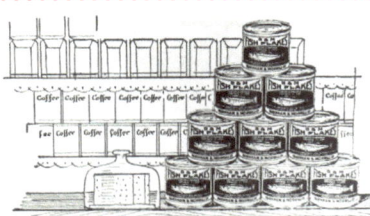

Put them on the counter every Thursday!

During Lent, display B & M FISH FLAKES and take the extra profit that the Season offers. B & M FISH FLAKES supply the Sea Food that your trade demands at this time. Selected Cod and Haddock, cooked, seasoned, broken into flakes ready for the table, and sealed in parchment lined tins, the same day they last the cold deep sea, from the cold deep sea.

Most grocers know the superiority of B & M Fish Flakes over other forms of Codfish. Every tin is guaranteed. Increase your business by displaying and recommending this wholesome and delicious Sea Food during Lent.

B & M FISH FLAKES
BURNHAM & MORRILL CO.
97 Water St. Portland, Me.

"Sales jumped to 10 cases a month . . .

when we put Jolly Time Pop Corn on the counter" *Says E. M. Schafer*

THE grocer in the picture is Mr. E. M. Schafer. E. M. and his brother John operate the famous Schafer Brothers store in the university section of Minneapolis, specializing in better class goods, and lines that show a real profit. They buy Jolly Time Hulless Pop Corn in ten-case lots.

"Jolly Time is a year-round seller with us," says E. M., "and getting it out where people can see it, has pushed our

sales up over ten cases a month in the winter season. There's room for a can or two of Jolly Time in nearly every order-bag these days, and by having Jolly time right on the counter, it's no effort to make the extra sale."

The experience of Schafer Brothers, duplicated in thousands of stores, has made Jolly Time the national leader in tinned pop corn. It is an extra-fine grade of corn, specially cleaned and cured to insure perfect popping condition, then hermetically sealed in tin to retain its freshness indefinitely. Being absolutely guaranteed to pop, and being familiar to millions through national advertising, Jolly Time is proving a rich source of extra profit for grocers.

It is well worth while to feature Jolly Time right now. Get it out where your customers can see it, and just see how fast your stock will turn.

FREE TO GROCERS
Let us send you a can of Jolly Time Brand Pop Corn free, so that you can try it out yourself. Let your family test it, too, and see if it doesn't beat any corn you've ever popped both in popping and in flavor. Simply clip this coupon, attach it to one of your sales slips or a letter head, write the name of your Jobber in the margin, and mail to us. Either Jolly Time with our compliments.

AMERICAN POP CORN COMPANY
World's Largest Exclusive Pop Corn Dealers
Box 784-L   Sioux City, Iowa

FIG. 1. Preserves and counters (Clockwise from top left: February 1926: 37; February 1926: 107; November 1929: 127; August 1929: 51)

A SPATIAL SHIFT

But *Progressive Grocer*'s attempt to list every benefit of canned foods makes all the more remarkable the magazine's complete omission of two major advantages. First, this type of packaging, stackable and durable, required less furniture and less-expensive display and storage fixtures than other products. Second and most important, because customers could handle cans themselves without risk of damage, and because the cans could be clearly labeled with their contents, brand name, and origin, canned goods could "sell themselves" and reduce the need for service. Either *Progressive Grocer*'s journalists were not yet aware of these benefits, or, more likely they were anxious not to disrupt the visceral attachment of the grocery industry to customer service and product substitution, as well as its hostility towards brand names that reduced its place and freedom. Regardless of the reasoning, *Progressive Grocer* in the 1920s avoided the most distinctive marketing appeals of the product they wanted to promote.

Can manufacturers and canners did "push" these benefits, but with extreme caution. In advertisements (Figure 1), most of the cans appear only behind the counter, in the old-fashioned way according to the traditional routine of grocer-mediated sales. The advertisers who designed these advertisements were well aware that most businesses were still working this way, so that it was prudent not to go too far against common practice, "all other groceries being equal," so to speak. Yet, in all these ads that use the same rhetoric, it is clear that the cans also highlight their ability to be stacked without need for shelves as well as their labels, which advertise their content and "speak" at the same time or in place of the grocer. Thus, by virtue of their superior "display" ability, the cans may slip surreptitiously and silently from the background shelves to the talkative foreground of the counter, and thus relegate the grocer in the middle, between the sales counter of old and the self-service system to come. This evolution continued through merchandising innovations like those of the Libby's Cannery (Figure 2).

In this advertisement, Libby's takes a step further. The staging is the same, with the double exposure of cans on shelves or in a stack, and the presence of the grocer. However, the counter, now useless, has disappeared, causing subtle changes: by moving to the ground, the pile of cans has grown; in jumping on the other side of the counter, the stacked or shelved cans have become fully accessible to customers. Thus, as we gradually discover, the can initiated the era of self-service in small and traditional grocery stores in the 1920s rather than in the larger, subsequent supermarkets. Of course, the transition is conservative: the grocer is retained, but his stacking gesture is clearly reversible into a taking one and transferable on the client's side: the purpose is to "gently"

"Our sales show a 25% increase yearly for 8 years with this plan"

writes L. DeVos, of Seattle, Wash.

A BUSINESS increase of over 250% in the last eight years! This is the record set by Mr. L. DeVos, Seattle merchant.

Much of the growth of the DeVos Stores, now four in number, he attributes to his sound merchandising policy on canned foods.

Starting in 1920, Mr. DeVos adopted a very definite plan. He concentrated on one line of canned foods which he knew would sell all comers. Each item of which could be depended upon to bring repeat sales—to help sell other items in the line.

"We chose the largest and most complete line of canned foods packed by one canner under one label," he writes.

"A quality line backed by big-scale national advertising—Libby's 100 Foods.

"We carry them complete from Canned Meats to Dried Fruits.

"Our business has shown a steady increase of 25% each year for the past eight years under this simple plan.

"We further find that our local advertising of three, six and dozen can lots of the items featured in Libby's current national advertising frequently doubles our sales on those foods over a thirty day period."

Mr. DeVos' plan, used successfully by thousands of other grocers, is a simple, practical one for increasing your profit and sales on canned foods. It is known as the Libby Idea. For free particulars, tear out this page, attach to your letterhead and mail today. Libby, McNeill & Libby, Dept. Q-22, Welfare Bldg., Chicago.

One of the DeVos Stores, Seattle, Washington, featuring the Libby Line

RADIO!

The Libby Hour is broadcast twice weekly over a great NBC Coast-to-coast chain of powerful stations.

TUESDAY evenings:
8:30 Eastern Time
7:30 Central Time
6:30 Mountain Time
5:30 Pacific Time

WEDNESDAY mornings:
10:45 Eastern Time
9:45 Central Time
11:15 Mountain Time
10:15 Pacific Time

Tune in — your customers do!

FIG. 2. Libby's plan (November 1929: 6-7)

---

teach grocers that cans are not only stackable as highlighted by the previous ads, but that they can also be left to the direct manipulation of clients, without having to fear that such manipulation generates material risks (they are solid) or health hazards (they are hermetic).

All in all, the strength and sealing of cans greatly supported the advent of self-service, while their opacity supported the invention of a new transparency, that of packaging, which paradoxically enabled the consumer to learn more about each product by its outer label than through a direct contact with it, by means of the statements of its composition and origin (Frohlich, 2011); and second to bypass the mediation of the vendor, which before was almost mandatory (Strasser, 1989).

Thus, the generalization of cans is inseparable from the promotion of brands like Libby's (November 1929: 6-7), Monarch (August 1929: 62-63), or Gerber's (January 1930: 74-75) and from the emergence of new preferences, like the taste for vitamins (March 1937: 10; March 1941: 142-143; September 1942: 97). The "pico-infrastructure" of cans clearly prepared the move of the grocery store to self-service and mass consumption, "for better (the rise of canners' and grocers' profits) or for worse (the strengthening of a chauvinist consumerism)," as one says at weddings, along with other promises of long, happy life, with many children, but also with even more cans: 788 cans a year for the average bride in 1953 (Figure 3)! ■

Acknowledgements: I warmly thank Progressive Grocer for granting me the permission to reproduce the images this publication rests upon.

FRANCK COCHOY *is Professor of sociology at the University of Toulouse, a member of the CERTOP-CNRS, France. He works in the field of economic sociology, with a focus on the human and technical mediations that frame the relationship between supply and demand.*

FIG. 3. A bride's future: opening 788 cans a year (July 1953: 51)

REFERENCES

Anderson, O. E. Jr. 1953. *Refrigeration in America*. Princeton: Princeton University Press.

Frohlich, X. Z. 2011. "Accounting for Taste: Regulating Food Labeling in the 'Affluent Society,' 1945–1995." PhD dissertation, Departments of History, Anthropology, and Science, Technology and Society, Massachusetts Institute of Technology, June.

Hine, T. 1995. *The Total Package: The Evolution and Secret Meanings of Boxes, Bottles, Cans, and Tubes*. Boston: Little, Brown and Co.

Strasser, S. 1989. *Satisfaction Guaranteed: The Making of the American Mass Market*. New York: Pantheon Books.

Twede, D. 2012. "The Birth of Modern Packaging: Cartons, Cans and Bottles." *Journal of Historical Research in Marketing* 4(2): 245–72.

The *Secret Lives* of *Corporate Food*

BIG COMPANIES ARE NOT JUST TRACING THEIR PRODUCTS' LIFE STORIES, BUT TELLING THEM TOO. **SUSANNE FREIDBERG** EXPLORES WHY.

DEEP INSIDE THE WALMART WEBSITE, a page opens with a question you would not expect from the world's biggest retailer:

How much do you know about what's behind a product's label?

It is not a quiz, merely a rhetorical hook. What Walmart really wants to talk about is how much it now knows about what's behind the label, and how it aims to use this knowledge to improve the "sustainability" of everything it sells. Exactly what Walmart means by this term the page itself does not explain. But it does link to a short and intriguingly titled video, "The Secret Life of Sliced Turkey."

Walmart has actually made several videos about its products' secret lives, all available on YouTube. All focus on food or its packaging (one explores the secret life of Walmart's recycled pizza boxes), all take viewers back into the supply chain, and all start from "the raw truth," as "Sliced Turkey" puts it, that the system producing these goods is fundamentally unsustainable. But the secrets revealed about sliced turkey are not the nasty ones uncovered in typical food documentaries. The video instead showcases little-known instances of innovation and cooperation. It's like a poultry industry exposé, flipped sunny-side up. Even the turkeys look happy.

Driving the video's cheery storyline is the knowledge produced by a modeling technique called life cycle assessment (LCA). LCA quantifies the environmental impacts incurred during a product's material "life," from raw material extraction through disposal. Although the technique dates back to the early 1970s, for years it received little attention outside of northern European engineering schools. Companies that hoped to use life cycle studies for green marketing found them slow, costly, often inconclusive, and all too contestable. A high-profile public relations war between the cloth and disposable diaper industries in the early 1990s

was just one of many instances when conflicting LCA studies raised more doubts than they resolved.

Today, though, corporate interest in LCA is booming, especially in the food business. Advances in method and software have streamlined the modeling of product life cycles, while the rise of an LCA professional community—the subject of my own ethnographic research—has boosted the technique's scientific credibility. Many of the world's biggest food companies have employed teams of LCA experts to "footprint" their products (the word has become a verb). They are quantifying farm-to-fork impacts not just on climate, but also water, land, air, and natural resources. At least for some, LCA has become part of the information infrastructure used both to manage global supply chains and to demonstrate transparency. Companies do not, however, necessarily intend to reveal their findings via advertising or labels. If they did, more people would have seen the "Sliced

Turkey" video. At last count, it had had fewer than 4,000 views on YouTube.

Why, exactly, do companies want to know about their products' secret lives? More to the point: why, and for whom, has Walmart made videos showing how much *it* knows about these lives? "Sliced Turkey" provides some clues. The only speaking role goes to an executive at Plumrose USA, the supplier of Walmart-brand sliced turkey. He observes that many people assume that such a product simply travels from farm to processor to store shelf. But the "whole story," he says, "involves much, much more." This is one of LCA's biggest selling points. While many green claims take account only of where or how goods are produced (i.e., local, organic), LCA allows companies to say they have looked at the *big picture*. The scale of analysis is itself authoritative.

This authority mirrors the vast geographic scope and complexity of many product supply chains. In the case of Walmart sliced turkey, the Plumrose

executive points out that every ingredient—not just turkey meat, but also salts, starch, and even the package zipper—"has a life of its own." As he explains how his company tracked all those lives, the video zooms out to show each as a brightly colored line, connecting Plumrose's Michigan headquarters to suppliers around the globe.

These lines then morph into a bar graph showing that turkey processing (aka slaughtering) accounts for the heaviest water use. In LCA terminology, it is a "hotspot." Often the hotspots identified by LCA defy popular assumptions. Life cycle studies of many foods, for instance, find that the farm, not transport or packaging, accounts for the bulk of many impacts (Tobler et al. 2001). Sliced turkey's water hotspot is no surprise; slaughter is a messy business, even if does not look that way in the Walmart video. This part of the story instead tells how Plumrose's findings inspired its turkey meat processor, Farbest Foods, to find a way to reduce its

Farmers especially must be prepared to show that they can produce sustainable food the Walmart way: more with less, for less.

 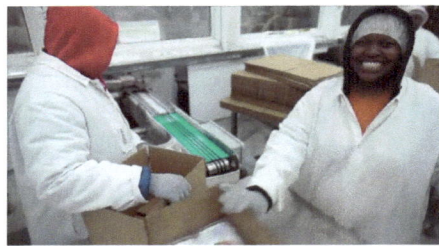 

water use by 50 million gallons of water per year.

The video then turns to a series of innovations undertaken by Plumrose at its own manufacturing facility, the hotspot for energy use. Viewers learn that the company's new trucks are up to 30 percent more efficient than their predecessors, and driving 800,000 less miles per year: "that's 300 less coast-to-coast hauls!" says the narrator (assuming roughly 3000 miles per haul, it would be closer to 160 hauls, but no matter). It has redesigned its packaging, cutting cardboard use by 35 percent even while selling more turkey. And it has switched to reusable pallets, saving 17,000 trees and 9 million gallons of water annually. Waving truck drivers, smiling workers, and sunny treetops fill the screen, but just as backdrop. The numbers are the message, especially the final one: Plumrose's innovations save the company nearly a million dollars per year.

LCA excels at numbers. Its "big picture" findings are composed entirely of quantitative data points. Although often highly approximate, these numbers lend themselves to forms of visualization and commensuration that in turn lend authority to LCA itself, at least in corporate circles. In contrast to fuzzy claims about a product's naturalness and eco-friendliness, LCA's bar graphs and pie charts appear to represent "just the facts" about its environmental impacts. LCA findings can also be converted into monetary values, demonstrating how much a specific eco-efficiency would save or cost. Indeed, one of the main reasons Walmart began collecting information about product life cycles was to identify ways to make them cheaper as well as greener. It indicated that it would be in suppliers' interest both to share their numbers on energy use, emissions, and so forth, and to make sure those numbers improved.

Near the end of "Sliced Turkey," the Plumrose executive returns, describing how his company's new perspective on its supply chain has proven "a real game-changer."

It's helping us grow our partnership with Walmart, it's showing us who the real leaders are in the industry and our supply chain, and it's helping us reduce costs. And perhaps more importantly, it's helping us make connections all the way back to the farm, where we know a lot of innovation opportunities exist.

What kind of innovations? A scene of fluffy turkey chicks offers no answers. This is probably no accident; LCA studies of poultry products show that the surest way to improve their eco-efficiency is to minimize the space, time and feed used to produce them (Leinonen et al. 2012). By certain measures, then, caged production systems rate better than free-range alter-

ALL PHOTOS FROM *THE SECRET LIFE OF SLICED TURKEY*

natives. But they do not make for the best video footage.

Although the Plumrose executive continues talking about partnership, he has already said all he needs. It's now clear that the intended audience for "Sliced Turkey" is not Walmart's consumers, but rather its suppliers, and in turn their suppliers. Farmers especially must be prepared to show that they can produce sustainable food the Walmart way: more with less, *for* less. After all, the narrator concludes, "in the end this is all about the consumer. It's about saving her money, and making sure that every dollar she spends is a vote for a better world."

Make no mistake: LCA can generate valuable insights into food's ecological life. It has already drawn attention to the less-visible impacts of fertilizer and feed production, as well as waste across the food chain. It has helped question the easy assumptions of locavorism. Whether the knowledge produced by LCA can help

make food measurably more sustainable depends, of course, on the measures and how they are used. LCA's claim to a "big picture" perspective already faces challenges from those who see important measures missing. Biodiversity, animal welfare, labor; LCA practitioners themselves admit that their models cannot yet capture many of the diverse and localized impacts of food's farm-to-fork existence. But they might someday. "The Secret Life of Sliced Turkey," in other words, may be in for a remake, and next time Walmart may not control the storyline. ■

SUSANNE FREIDBERG *is Professor of Geography at Dartmouth College and the author of* Fresh: A Perishable History.

REFERENCES

Leinonen, I., A. G. Williams, , J. Wiseman, J. Guy, and I. Kyriazakis. 2012. "Predicting the Environmental Impacts of Chicken Systems in the United Kingdom through a Life Cycle Assessment: Egg Production Systems." *Poultry Science* 91(1):26–40. doi:10.3382/ps.2011-01635.

Tobler, C., V. H. M. Visschers, and M. Siegrist. 2011. "Organic Tomatoes versus Canned Beans: How Do Consumers Assess the Environmental Friendliness of Vegetables?" *Environment and Behavior* doi:10.1177/0013916510372865.

The Art of the

How do cheesemongers extend the value of a dying commodity? **Heather Paxson** explores how mongers care for living cheese—and for the craft of their trade.

Monger

monger, *n*. **1.** *a*. A merchant, trader, dealer, or trafficker (freq. of a specified commodity); (from the 16th cent.) a person engaged in a petty or disreputable trade or traffic. Sometimes short for an established compound such as cheesemonger, where the context makes this clear.
—*Oxford English Dictionary*

Cheese is alive with microorganisms: bacteria, yeasts, and molds whose metabolizing action on the sugars and proteins in milk generates the aromas and flavors and textures that say "cheese" to us. The process of cheese "becoming" does not end once curd is separated from whey and pressed into molds; it continues through the alchemy of ripening. Indeed, cheeses are never *done* ripening; they continue to mature until they are eaten and digested, or—if too far gone—tossed out fully to rot. Cheese's mutability makes it a challenging, but also potentially quite satisfying, item to retail. This essay elaborates on the contemporary art of artisanal cheese retail.

I am not talking about plastic-encased rectangles of supermarket cheese chilling alongside cartons of milk and yogurt in tall dairy cases along the back walls of superstores. That cheese requires a different story, one that begins with the mid-nineteenth century move of American cheesemaking off the farm and into cooperatively owned factories where farmers pooled their milk to be processed by hired craftsmen. Variability remained an issue until the introduction of pasteurization in the 1930s, an innovation adopted for market reasons of consistency, standardization, and economies of scale; pasteurization meant that cheese could be safely made from older milk that had traveled greater distances. Today, cheese destined for the dairy case (or a pizza, for that matter) is fabricated using automated machinery and molded in 40-pound blocks that are immediately encased in protective plastic to prevent bacteria and molds from growing on their surface during ripening. The history of cheesemaking's industrialization is a tale of gaining mastery over cheese's organic variability as a means of scaling up production and extending shelf life.

Artisanally manufactured cheese embodies different values. It is made in relatively small batches using minimal technology and often, increasingly so in the United States since the 1980s, on the dairy farms that provide the milk. Such cheeses may be allowed to age in the open air, even resting on wooden boards conducive to the very microbial colonization of their surfaces that vacuum packaging is intended to avoid. Artisanal cheeses do not "go moldy" so much as they develop "natural rinds," which require a good deal of sustained human labor in "turning" (e.g., flipping over), "washing," (rubbing down with a brine solution) and brushing the cheeses for months on end to develop. Those rinds—and hence the appearance, taste, and desirability of the cheese—vary from producer to producer, from batch to batch, and from wheel to wheel. It takes skill not only to make such cheese, but also to sell it. Unlike traders of standardized commodities who sell almost exclusively on competitive pricing, specialized cheese retailers, known as cheesemongers, trade in goods whose value is invested in connoisseurship (Gewertz and Errington 2010:68). Mongers' knowledge of the vagaries of cheese—how it's made, by whom, how it will behave in one's fridge, how best to serve it, even when a cheese is most itself (*à point*, the French say)—can enhance the commercial value of a good.

Call it crafty, call it craft: skilled, reputable cheesemongers move cheese in varying states of decomposition to trusting customers. As David, a young cheesemonger, said to me, "All my cheeses are ticking time clocks." Perishability creates a drag on merchants' profitability. David is in the business of selling cheese, as much of it as he can. His maximization strategy is based not on pushing quantity (he wants people to buy cheese they can consume within a day or two), but instead on expanding notions of quality. To mitigate loss by enhancing his inventory's quality, David's work is both practical and discursive. The *practical* job is to slow down the transformation of a cheese's organoleptic qualities by retarding ripening and heading off rotting. Here, commercial infrastructure of refrigeration and humidity control join David's practical knowledge of cheese care. The *discursive* job is to convey to consumers an appreciation for "real" (i.e., nonindustrial) cheese's fundamental instability so that they know not to expect absolute fidelity in a cheese's sensory qualities.

First, to stabilize those material qualities as much as possible, David tends to his cheeses with care ("I'm like an old Jewish mother who worries too much about her kids," he told me). In the shop, each piece on display is rewrapped daily before being returned to refrigerated cases. Any mold growth appearing on the cut surface of a wheel is scraped off with a knife. The rinds of hard-aged cheeses, kept for weeks or even months in refrigerator cases in the back of the shop, are brushed and patted to remove cheese mites or excess mold growth. Brooklyn-based cheese seller Brad Dubé calls this, in studiously simplistic terms, "cheese care," explaining in an interview:

> It's what a cheese monger has always done. Cheese doesn't always travel well. The job of the monger has always been to receive the cheese, assess it, and decide what they're going to do with it to present it best to the consumer. That means that sometimes you have to do what we—the old

A weekly bulletin from the shop where David works (it's primarily a wine store) once recounted the craziness of catching the cheesemonger in the act of smearing butter on a cheese, as if cheese needed the extra fat! When I mentioned this to David, he laughed at the joke. The cheese was a Caciocavallo from Sicily and the rind had cracked in transit; David described the crack as a "wound" that can open the cheese to microbial infection, so he filled it with a bit of butter, "like a band-aid." He'd learned the trick from a colleague while working on the other side of town.

Such routine yet skilled care of an already-aged cheese is not to be confused with what the French call *affinage*, or "finishing." The *affineur*, a professional cheese-ripener, acquires young or "green" wheels of cheese and undertakes their ripening from the beginning. As Dubé would have it, cheese care aims at maintaining a cheese as the producer intended it, whereas *affinage* purposefully influences what a cheese might become. Such value-adding labor is increasingly being done in specialty shops in the United States. A retail-based *affineur* might add a locally brewed beer—say, Brooklyn Brewery Local 2—to a brine solution spritzed on the surface of a young cheese that has come into the store. In just such a way, Kinderhook Creek, Old Chatham Sheeperding Company's mold-ripened cheese, becomes C-Local, a treat only to be found at Murray's Cheese in Manhattan, where the yeasty transmogrification takes place. For practitioners of routine cheese care to lay claim to the art of *affinage*—a question raised by a *New York Times* story in 2011 (Gordinier 2011)—is for many mongers an unseemly affectation. And yet it raises an interesting question: who should take credit for making the cheese what it becomes by the point of sale?

For all David's concerted efforts to slow down ripening, the cheeses, of course, continue to develop, which is to say change. This is where the discursive labor comes in. To sell a cheese that is never exactly as it was before, David *narrates* a cheese's qualities as continuously dynamic, such that different qualities (taste, ooziness, odor) might be temporarily stabilized for a given cheese at each point of sale (see Callon et al. 2002). He works to convince customers that one of the charms of artisanal cheese is that the "same" cheese will never *be* the same, owing to its aliveness (i.e., perishability). In addition to cheese care, then, David practices customer care.

In order to sell an unfinished commodity—one whose material qualities are not only shape-shifting but whose *value* remains culturally and economically underdetermined, a little bit suspect—David encourages customers to reevaluate their judgments. "Last time you didn't like the Rupert? Try it again" (meaning, try this one, right

now), "it's aged out little more" (or, it's younger). When I say, "I like Hooligan," a raw-milk, washed-rind cheese made by Mark Gillman in Connecticut, what I mean is that I like the range of qualities that generally characterizes Hooligan at a particular stage in its life: I would never buy Hooligan without trying a taste from the piece I'm considering purchasing. To me, the cheese is a bit bland when too young and rather off-putting when too ripe; I want to hit my sweet spot. And it's my spot to hit. Unlike European classics, when it comes to American artisanal cheeses, there is no *à point*. Who knows when a Hooligan is perfectly itself? There is no ideal type for a cheese named and made by a single artisan (another way in which American artisanal cheeses are "unfinished" as commodities). There are qualities that a particular piece of cheese may embody, and consumers who may appreciate those qualities. David's job as monger is to play matchmaker.

Flavor preference isn't merely idiosyncratic. David also frames the sense-able qualities of a cheese at hand as being good *for* various purposes and taste experiences. Consider a mold-ripened pyramid of goat's milk cheese that, at its peak, might be nice on a cheese plate. As it "ages out," its flavor can become ammoniated; its desiccated paste hardens. In this state, David explains to customers, the cheese can be "shaved" to add flavor in cooking or to salads. Illustrating this to me, he pointed to Sophia, an ash-ribboned, mold-ripened goat's milk cheese made by Judy Schad in Indiana. David buys cheese directly from Judy; to rationalize shipping costs, he must order a sizeable amount per shipment. For this to be viable on a counter as small as his, he must sell Judy's cheese at different moments in its life course: young, mature, and rather elderly. As a commodity good, David sells Sophia at different stages of being "finished."

Is this simply cheese care, what good cheesemongers do as standard practice to trade in unfinished commodities? Or is it new-school *affinage*, turning someone else's craft product into something unintended? Is it customer care, imparting the knowledge of a connoisseur, or is it a sleight-of-hand trick to get wealthy customers to part with more of their money? At stake is whether cheesemongering should be recognized as a skilled craft, or whether it deserves the taint of disreputable trade, which is one of the meanings of *mongering* listed in the Oxford English Dictionary. And that question depends more broadly on the status of artisanship in an industrial economy. For producers and mongers alike, it is a marginal status, financially tenuous and prone to romanticization: and thus also morally suspect (Paxson 2013).

Questions of *scale* haunt both. "How Big Is Big Enough (Without Getting Too Big)?" "Is Scaling Up Selling Out?" These panel sessions at meetings of the American Cheese Society I've attended were organized by and for producers, but they could speak equally well to many retailers' concerns. Can small retailers of artisanal goods scale up? Well, sure they can. Manhattan's Murray's Cheese stocks deli case outposts in Kroger supermarkets. Does scaling up effect the condition of the cheese as it's presented to potential consumers? Of course it does. Wedges prewrapped in plastic will never match the condition of cut-and-wrap: but then again, cut-and-wrap at my local Whole Foods Market is not the same as buying cheese from David's cheese counter. It's not just that David is more knowledgeable; his cheese is in noticeably better shape, in part because he's handling a smaller inventory. And—surprise!—David's cheese is not any more expensive for me to purchase. Retail mirrors production: larger retail operations move more product and generate greater corporate profit, while smaller operations that work "by hand" and offer a more intimate shopping experience see lower profit margins. At the same time, "little guy" status generates customer loyalty for retail shops as well as for craft producers. Regular customers, after all, trust "their" mongers to steer them toward the best cheeses, not just the ones that are overstocked or may be reaching the point of no return, which, with cheese, is always a possibility. For many cheesemongers, participation in this sort of economy of sentiment—more than the possibility of increasing profit—makes mongering a job worth doing. ■

HEATHER PAXSON *is Associate Professor of Anthropology at the Massachusetts Institute of Technology, and author of* The Life of Cheese: Crafting Food and Value in America *(University of California Press, 2013).*

REFERENCES

Callon, Michel, Cécile Méadel, and Vololona Rabeharisoa. 2002. "The Economy of Qualities." *Economy and Society* 31(2):194–217.

Gewertz, Deborah and Frederick Errington. 2010. *Cheap Meat: Flap Food Nations in the Pacific Islands.* Berkeley: University of California Press.

Gordinier, Jeff. 2011. "Cheese: A Coming of Age Story." *New York Times*, October 4. http://www.nytimes.com/2011/10/05/dining/cheese-and-affinage-a-coming-of-age-story.html?_r=1&ad xnnl=1&pagewanted=all&adxnnlx=1386626524-aiS9w6sT60ST067i1S5OOg.

Hobbs, Peter. 2011. "Fromage Fight? NY Times Article Touches A Nerve in the Cheese Community." *Nona Brooklyn: What's Good Today?* [blog], October 16. http://nonabrooklyn.com/fromage-fight-new-york-times-article-touches-nerve-in-the-cheese-community/#.Up6aeI1Ppqk.

Paxson, Heather. 2013. *The Life of Cheese: Crafting Food and Value in America.* Berkeley: University of California Press.

REFRIGERATION The number of grocery stores in Guatemala doubled in the 1990s, also transforming in character. Whereas Guatemalan supermarkets once provided high-end luxury goods, they now focus on mass-produced, processed foods. A massive store, today owned by Walmart, was a short walk from the public hospital obesity clinic where I worked. As depicted in the photograph, many of its goods required refrigeration.

Refrigerator Units, Normal Goods

Emily Yates-Doerr tells two stories that reveal the challenge of grasping global inequality.

IN THE WINDBURNED OUTSKIRTS of Guatemala's second largest city is a track of half-built homes. It is early 2008, before investors stop believing that the future lies in housing. But even now the future has cast its shadow on the development. People do not realize it yet, but the flow of capital for construction has dried up, and the rows of concrete structures partially assembled will remain that way.

Still, the marketers have not yet walked away, and tall billboards throughout the city advertise the homes with images of happy families gathered around dining room tables, mothers at work in their modern kitchens. This is the first generation of housing built this way. In the older design, several families—or perhaps they are a single family; here, units are difficult to disaggregate—circled

around a common hearth, sharing stews served from large communal bowls. In contrast, the kitchens on the billboards feature the requisite assets of progress: the kitchen, intended for a nuclear family, is separated from other rooms in the house, with a gas oven and a tall refrigerator.

After several months of ethnographic fieldwork studying obesity at the regional public hospital, I first make my way to the housing development where a few families have begun to live. I am there to learn about what happens outside the nutrition clinic, which is a place where (mostly) women stand on scales to measure their BMI—the ratio of mass to height that correlates, according to both the United Nations and doctors in the region, to their health. The scales seem to be failing: most obviously, many are broken or difficult to

calibrate; but also, they diagnose as overweight people whose narratives are filled with hunger, and the resultant advice—to eat less—does not make much sense to anyone involved.

Doña Monterroso had been to the clinic several times, and we had become familiar. When I asked if I might visit her at her home, she gave me an address that brought me to the development. The nearest bus route passed some distance from her home, and then there was the walk past quiet buildings where pavement turned to gravel. Like other houses, hers was unfinished: rooms missing doors, windows covered with plastic where there might have been glass. Still, there was soup boiling on the gas stove. And featured prominently in the dimly lit kitchen was the refrigerator. While I watched Doña Monterroso carefully finish preparing the meal—which she then offered graciously to me though I had brought her nothing—I noticed the refrigerator was not plugged in, and was used only for storage.

Doña Monterroso did not believe that it was capable of cooling, and whether it was or not was beside the point since this potential had no potential here. The developers' vision reached further than the necessary cables, and electricity was erratic. Not that it mattered, since electricity was too expensive and she could not carry enough food from the market to have to worry it would spoil. Tortillas, beans, vegetables, or broth not eaten in one meal were incorporated into the next and never went to waste. The storage space was useful enough, but she hadn't asked for the refrigerator.

I would eventually meet other women with refrigerators that served to store and not to cool. And I would learn that many refrigerators come to Guatemala second-hand, arriving not through a consumer's demand to own but through a demand to get rid of an object that no one anywhere really wants any more. Refrigerators, along with a flood of other products, are exchanged in markets where demand is a misleading term, since the demand in question is less to own than to dispose. Refrigerators, especially old and broken ones, can leak toxic chemicals, and the North Americans who once bought them new do not want to keep them around.

I AM FAR FROM GUATEMALA, at a meeting on global health metrics and evaluation held in downtown Seattle, when I am reminded of Doña Monterroso's refrigerator. I am attending a panel focused on disease and global inequality, and though these are issues I care about, the inequality I encounter here is unlike that encountered in the Guatemalan clinic. There, measurement resulted in endless confusion, exacerbating stratifications in clinical care; here, inequality is a mathematical concept dependent upon measurement. When a speaker explains that refrigerators lie at the center of their calculations, I am struck that what is granted global significance, much like refrigerators

themselves, falls apart when made to travel. This is the story she tells:

Owning a boat in a landlocked country means something vastly different than it does in an island nation. Owning a cell phone today means something very dif-

---

THE STORAGE SPACE WAS USEFUL ENOUGH, BUT SHE HADN'T ASKED FOR THE REFRIGERATOR.

---

ferent with regards to wealth than it did twenty years ago.[1]

The speaker is highlighting for the audience the problem that many assets used by economists to measure wealth are not useful for making *global* calculations since their values shift so dramatically across space and time. Most who are listening know this. They are versed in econometrics: the language of this conference and of a field of study that has claimed the title "global public health." The room itself seems to nod when she explains that they must instead identify normal goods. Normal goods, in the parlance of this community, are goods that people everywhere are more likely to own as their wealth increases, and which can be used because of this predictability to, in her words, "anchor translations between surveys and global indices." Normal goods, she says, make scales hang together.

So boats and cell phones do not work, she says. But refrigerators do. The charts she shows correlating increased demand for them to increases in income look nearly identical whether depicting Afghanistan, Bangladesh, or the Côte d'Ivoire. Somewhere a surveyor has knocked on a door, perhaps tentatively asking the person who answers, among the other questions to be asked, do you own a refrigerator? Or maybe the surveyor can see the answer for himself and does not need to ask. He indicates yes or no on the paper he holds, then adds this to the stack of completed files that he carries by motorcycle, or bus, or even by foot if resources are scare enough, to an office where his marks are entered into computer spreadsheets. This can now be called data, the lead or ink of his encounter becoming a series of determinate zeros and ones.

If the refrigerator that is counted is broken, this is not relevant to the calculations here. The problem the speaker has identified pertains not to refrigerators but to the measure of wealth itself. Wealth is crude, with many jagged edges, and it does not slide easily enough from site to site. It gets caught. It slows the statisticians down, effacing their models as it does so. "Wealth doesn't make much sense to us," she tells the sympathetic audience. She, meanwhile, has found a way of translating data on refrigerators into units of dollars. Unlike the nonsense value of wealth, dollars are an ideal unit to work with since they can be cleanly aggregated and disaggregated, resulting in the now self-evident scales of local/small and global/big. From there, she can produce the desired single number that can account for the value of assets across place (standardized by the unit of country) and time (standardized by the unit of year).

The procedure is intricate, involving the Gini coefficient and statistical maneuvers sophisticated and skilled enough to win her the conference prize and, when she accepts it, a standing ovation. This is important work since it offers a set of tools for making values equivalent and thus comparable across landscapes that may not otherwise have much in common. It is only once equality has been established—the features of difference filed away—that they can "relate inequality back to health," which is, after all, the theme of the conference.

She reminds her audience that inequality is meaningless until it is made into a calculable unit. But once it is made measurable, there is much she can do. Using this full map and a few simple equations she can show that a country whose measure of inequality has recently increased has worse indicators for maternal health and childhood mortality. Her work offers evidence that inequality is an impediment to progress.

THESE TWO STORIES BOTH SUGGEST that inequality links tightly to progress; but from there, the conclusions sharply diverge. For econometric calculations would have it that more refrigerators would correspond to better health, and

---

1 The talk is available at http://ghme.org/global-and-national-burden-disease-iv.

in my work this kind of progress—and these kinds of numbers—are themselves a source of harm. The speaker seeks to convert asset data into a single measure, but refrigerators and the inequalities to which they refer are not everywhere the same. Freezing goods, from the mechanically deboned animal parts increasingly available in Guatemala to values themselves, does not enable them to travel unchanged. Refrigerators, taken by the global health community as evidence that people have been successfully inserted into the cold chains of global connection, are evidence in other communities of the very failure of these chains.

The speaker measures inequality using statistical techniques capable of erasing empty spaces—filling in holes to make a whole. My research has another intention. My case—an afternoon in the home of Doña Monterroso—is neither whole nor part. Though it is necessarily partial, a story selected with other stories that could be told, it does not aspire to totality. It is not a proxy for something else. Whereas the speaker aspires to create a map that is complete, I remain unsettled by the disappearance of those never counted. Her statistics make it so these gaps are not significant (a technical term). Signification is a very different thing for me. In my work, evidence is what makes the absent present rather than what enables it to disappear.

Inequality, as I encountered it in the obesity clinic in Guatemala, is not something to be calculated with a vision of equality as its opposing pole. It might be helpful to be reminded that a coefficient, the magic number upon which the speaker's technique is based, is a multiplier of a property. It is this practice of multiplication that allows the speaker to "translate from the individual survey to a global scale" (her words) and to ultimately use a refrigerator to make claims about inequality and health.

This is the terrain of what has come to be called Big Data, in which many small observations can be further replicated to draw big conclusions: where researchers translate between local and global scales with fast calculations. Meanwhile, in the daily life of the nutrition clinic, replication is not a good tactic. There, differences in histories and trajectories cannot be made equal, and not much comes quickly. My interactions did not translate between self-evident scales of small/local and large/global as if persons and places were units to be aggregated. In my research, scales just didn't seem to work very well. They left people frustrated and without meaningful care.

And as to the property that the coefficient multiplies? According to the speaker, asset data are "easily collected." Perhaps there are well-trained surveyors who are capable of confronting strangers with these awkward curiosities, but these questions have never been easy for me. I did not ask Doña Monterroso if she was paying rent or owned the house she lived in, or how much these things cost. Even if I could bring myself to ask people about the price of their property, I would treat their answers cautiously. Ownership—belonging, to use a salient anthropological term—is not a simple thing. In Guatemala, it is not uncommon to enter the house of a seemingly poor woman who opens her refrigerator and shares her meal. We can make calculations of this—no free lunch, as the saying goes, all has a price. But a result of making all values of health and wealth measurable is that clinicians tell hungry people to eat and weigh less and statisticians treat toxic, broken refrigerators as assets.

The expert-driven field of global health makes a powerful claim to evaluation, but as Doña Monterosso's refrigerator makes evident, there are other forms of evaluation and expertise with less-dazzling impact, but which remain powerful nonetheless. The field of global health is hard at work gathering and assembling its data. But data are not given. They come from stories. How might global public health be changed by working hard to gather, and making space to tell, more of those? ■

EMILY YATES-DOERR *is a postdoc at the Amsterdam Institute for Social Science Research of the University of Amsterdam. She is working on an ethnographic project on the formation of the UN's Sustainable Development Goals that documents how global health, agricultural, and economic interests converge over concerns for hunger, climate change, food price, and metabolic transitions.*

REFERENCES

Heuts, Frank, and Annemarie Mol. 2013. "What Is a Good Tomato? A Case of Valuing in Practice." *Valuation Studies* 1(2):125–46.

Law, John. 2004. "And If the Global Were Small and Noncoherent? Method, Complexity, and the Baroque." *Environment and Planning D: Society and Space* 22(1):13–26.

Martin, Emily. 2007. "Manic Markets." In *Bipolar Expeditions: Mania and Depression in American Culture*, 234–68. Princeton, NJ: Princeton University Press.

Merry, Sally Engle. 2011. "Measuring the World: Indicators, Human Rights, and Global Governance: with CA comment by John M. Conley." *Current Anthropology* 52(S3):S83–S95.

Pigg, Stacy Leigh. In Press. "On Sitting and Doing: Ethnography as Action in Global Health." *Social Science & Medicine* http://dx.doi.org/10.1016/j.socscimed.2013.07.018.

Strathern, Marilyn. 1999. "Puzzles of Scale." In *Property, Substance, and Effect: Anthropological Essays on Persons and Things*, 204–25. London, New Brunswick, NJ: Athlone Press.

Walter, Maggie, and Chris Anderson. 2013. *Indigenous Statistics: A Quantitative Research Methodology*, 159. Walnut Creek, CA: Left Coast Press.

PHOTO BY PETER CLARK

FAT/ CHOLESTEROL

MIKKO JAUHO DEMONSTRATES HOW A 'DOUBLE RISK OBJECT' CONNECTS THE WORLDS OF FOOD AND HEALTH ACROSS DIFFERENT SCALES.

IN A ROUTINE HEALTH EXAMINATION, I am diagnosed with high serum cholesterol. During a counseling session the public health nurse goes through the different cholesterol fractions. Since the overall cholesterol level exceeds the nationally defined limit of 5 mM, and despite the fact that my risk score (the sum of cholesterol and other risk factors like age, smoking, exercise, and blood pressure) is low, I am given detailed nutritional advice. The public health nurse exhorts me to avoid certain foods, to be careful with others, and to increase the consumption of yet a third group of foods. The goal is to reduce the intake of the so-called bad, hard, animal fats and increase the intake of good, soft, vegetable fats. I am recommended to use low-fat products, some of which have a specific sign granted by the Finnish Heart Association to heart-friendly products. These products contain less salt and fat or better types of fat compared with similar regular products. Should my high cholesterol persist and my other risk factors worsen as I get older, I might be prescribed a specific cholesterol-lowering medication.

EVEN THE VERY BORDERS OF NATURE AND CULTURE ARE REARRANGED THROUGH THE BREEDING OF THE "LOW-FAT PIG" WITH LEANER MEAT

THIS IS A TYPICAL SITUATION in contemporary affluent societies, faced by thousands of middle-aged and elderly persons every day. The post-World War II surge of cardiovascular diseases, together with an etiology that has implicated dietary fats and high serum cholesterol in their rise and a medical rationality centered on the notion of risk factors, has had a profound effect on patterns of food production and consumption as well as practices of medicine, public health, and personal health care. I argue that key to this assemblage is the fat/cholesterol double. It operates as a "risk object" (Hilgartner 1992), which guides efforts towards healthier eating and connects various arenas in the world of food and medicine across different scales.

In the world of food, regular surveys monitor the food consumption patterns of the population. They indicate that a large portion of consumers regularly take notice of the fat content of the foods they eat. Many have changed their eating habits into more health- or fat-conscious direction. Different nutritional sects argue what type of fat in what amount is beneficial or dangerous to your health. Government-appointed officials issue meticulously weighed recommendations on fat intake, which then guide food provisioning in various settings ranging from institutional kitchens to industrial product development and labeling. Supermarket shelves are bursting with low-fat and -calorie products. Notions of fat, risks, and health have also reorganized the agricultural sector, changing the structure of dairy production. Even the very borders of nature and culture are rearranged through the breeding of the "low-fat pig" with leaner meat or the introduction of genetically modified organisms (GMOs) into food production.

Moving over to the world of medicine, huge research efforts in biochemistry, medicine, and epidemiology are organized around fat and cholesterol to track the pathways of fat metabolism, uncover the functions of cholesterol in the body, or gauge the effects of cholesterol-lowering diets and medications to the morbidity and mortality of various populations. Numerous public health endeavors have been started to educate the consumers on the effects of a high-fat diet, to stress the importance of knowing one's serum cholesterol levels, and to engage consumers in the task of cholesterol reduction. A massive industry operates around pharmaceuticals that have been developed to medicate the risk represented by high cholesterol and to offer a shortcut to lowering it. There are also novel hybrids between the worlds of food and medicine in the form of functional foods, some of which are designated to lower serum cholesterol.

Hence, a few relatively simple molecules influence the operation of vast systems of food production, provision, and consumption, not to mention medicine, public health, and personal health care. In this sense, fat/cholesterol is a risk object with systemic effects.

However, there is more. It is interesting to note that this risk object is a *double*. Depending on the context, either cholesterol *or* (type of) fat is evoked. Thus, it is cholesterol that is measured and medicated, but fat that is produced, regulated, labeled, and consumed. I want to argue that it is precisely this double nature of fat/cholesterol that enables the continuous and flexible exchange across different scales between the various arenas in the worlds of food and medicine.

Take, for example, the labeling of various fats in food products. As a regulatory device, food labeling is geared to the idea of food as nutrition, nutrition as an avenue to personal health care, personal health care as the avoidance of future harms (i.e., risk reduction), and consumers as guardians of their individual risk profiles, which are established in the clinic. One key risk factor for cardiovascular health is serum cholesterol level. Hence, cholesterol in the clinic is connected to the fats in the products at the supermarket; food production, retailing, nutrition, and public health are all tied together through fat/cholesterol.

The fact that the lipid metabolism involves several types of cholesterol or cholesterol-carrying lipoproteins—HDL, LDL, and VLDL—and several types of fat or fatty acids—saturated, polyunsaturated, monounsaturated, and ω-3, ω-6, and ω-9—complicates the picture and enables new types of exchanges, but does not change the basic situation. In some arenas, when the scale of observation is kept small, cholesterol fractions or types of fat are taken into account; in some arenas with a more crude scale, they are not. For example, when researching fat metabolism, fats and cholesterol are broken down into even more specific entities. In the clinic, when taking a blood test, the various cholesterol fractions are differentiated and the HDL/LDL relation is calculated, but recommendations are still often (erroneously) based on the total cholesterol value. Similarly, labeling practices list different types of fat on the food products, types of fat have different properties, and many animal foods contain both types of fats. Still, everyday parlance typically resorts to the crude distinction between animal/hard and vegetable/soft fats.

The coupling of cholesterol/fat as a double risk object has resulted from longstanding frailties in the etiological chain from dietary fat via serum cholesterol and arteriosclerosis to infarction. The documentation of the transition from (the amount and type of) dietary fat to serum cholesterol levels in particular has proved to be problematic. On biochemical and physiological levels, the influence of fats on cholesterol metabolism and the role of cholesterol in arteriosclerosis are well documented. Similarly, in small-scale clinical interventions, serum cholesterol has been lowered successfully by a low-fat diet. The picture gets trickier when the scale gets bigger. Population studies have established connections among the fat content of diet, blood cholesterol levels, and cardiovascular and/or total morbidity and mortality. Unfortunately, not all studies have found significant links. The situation is even worse for mass intervention studies that have sought to establish a statistically significant connection between risk-factor reduction and benefits for morbidity and mortality. Several lengthy and costly large-scale epidemiological studies failed to show the link. It was only the introduction of cholesterol-lowering drugs into research that managed to deliver the necessary evidence on the health benefits of cholesterol reduction. Significantly, the results from the drug trials were then extrapolated on diet, providing the ultimate scientific evidence on which nutritional recommendations of fat use rest. (Aronowitz 1998:111–44; Garrety 1997; Greene 2007). This testifies to the ongoing difficulty of crossing the dietary fat/serum cholesterol threshold, and the central role of the cholesterol/fat double in upholding the current heart disease prevention regime.

Fresh out of the clinic with my diet recommendations, I am wondering how a simple test result, built around a fundamentally arbitrary threshold value, can influence my and others' lives in such a profound way. Personally I will probably ignore the advice for now: after all, my HDL/LDL ratio and triglycerides levels were okay according to the test results. But I will be keeping an eye on my cholesterol, maybe testing it on a regular basis. Most likely I will be more diligent when choosing what to eat, observing the fat content of different foods at the supermarket and in the restaurant. Maybe I will also exercise a bit more, just to be on the safe side. Thus, I will be joining the millions who feel anxiety about their future health and manage their risk factors in a preemptive way, thereby paying tribute to the double risk object of fat/cholesterol. ∎

MIKKO JAUHO *is a Senior Researcher at the National Consumer Research Centre Finland. He is currently working on the history of health risks, cardiovascular diseases and dietary fats.*

REFERENCES

Aronowitz, Robert A. 1998. *Making Sense of Illness: Science, Society, and Disease.* Cambridge, UK: Cambridge University Press.

Garrety, Karin. 1997. "Social Worlds, Actor-Networks and Controversy: The Case of Cholesterol, Dietary Fat and Heart Disease." *Social Studies of Science* 27(5): 727–73.

Greene, Jeremy A. 2007. *Prescribing by Numbers: Drugs and the Definition of Disease.* Baltimore, MD: The Johns Hopkins University Press.

Hilgartner, Stephen. 1992. "The Social Construction of Risk Objects: Or, How to Pry Open Networks of Risk." In *Organizations, Uncertainties, and Risk,* edited by James F. Short and Lee Clarek, 39–53. Boulder, CO: Westview.

The Oil Palm Kernel and the Tinned Can

Do you see the peculiar industrial legacy of West Africa's oil palm tree in a humble tin can? Makalé Faber-Cullen does.

MICHEL FABER LIKED TO HAVE A GLASS OF RUM after balancing the day's ledgers. The shop doors had long been locked and his office, a tidy nook behind a wall of paned merchandise cabinets, was where he sipped Rhum Agricole Martinique. The rum was a treat, reserved for when he helmed the country's flagship general store near our family home on the salty, bustling peninsula of Conakry, Guinea.

It was the 1930s, and *rhum agricole*, soap, tinned milk, pâté, bolts of fabric, casks of wine, watches, medicines, stationery, nails, gasoline, candles, tobacco, sugar, biscuits, margarine, and more arrived by boat for distribution to the 12 stores and factories throughout Guinea that my SuSu grandpère Michel managed for his colonial employers, Marseilles-based Compagnie française de l'Afrique occidentale (CFAO).

CFAO ships deposited goods produced and packaged in France (la Métropole and its colonies). Then, into those same hulls went Guinea's bananas, rubber, leather, wood, pepper, ivory, coffee, gold, and the oily seeds of sesame, peanut, and palm (CFAO 1900:26). Of this shifting assemblage floating back and forth across the Atlantic Ocean, palm oil and palm kernel oil stand out for having, quite literally, greased the wheels of England's Industrial Revolution.

As historian Martin Lynn explains in *Commerce and Economic Change in West Africa*, palm oil was used in the manufacture of Europe's (and Britain's) soap and candles, in textile trades, and as a lubricant for railroads and industrial machinery (Lynn 2002:3, 46). But its most interesting use, in my view, was as an ingredient in tinning—the process of thinly coating sheets of iron or steel with tin to prevent rusting. This process accelerated one of the most transformative food access innovations: tin cans. Preserving foodstuffs in tin meant reliable nourishment well beyond a harvest, thereby addressing a constant challenge faced by our species. Arguably, the availability of tinned food expanded empires and recalibrated human settlement patterns and diets. Meat, fish, fruit, biscuits, vegetables, cigarettes, and sweeteners all have been tinned at one point or another and made available to workers, picnickers, soldiers, and travelers alike.

Palm oil's role in tinning was inceptive and specific:

> *After the second bath in sulphuric acid the [metal] sheets remain in water until ready for tinning. Standing in front of the dresser are three men, known as the tinman, the washman, and the riser. They are flanked by several girls, called "branners" and "cleaners." Into the first pot containing boiling palm oil, the tinman places the sheets one by one and leaves them immersed from one to five minutes in order to clean the surface of all impurities and make it absorbent. Next, he transfers the sheets to the second pot which holds molten tin. They remain immersed from two to five minutes, and their surface forms an amalgam with the tin (Dunbar 1915:10).*

The foods preserved in tin cans, in turn, were inserted into regional diets across the globe. I'm thinking here of the great Spam, bean, and evaporated milk diasporas. When we look down grocery store aisles, lined floor-to-ceiling with canned foods, we are seeing the peculiar industrial legacy of West Africa's great oil palm, *Elaies guineensis*.

While the oil palm is now found in Southeast Asia and South America, it is indigenous to Africa, flourishing between 7 degrees north and south of the equator with its greatest concentration in West Africa between Sierra Leone and Congo (Lynn 2002:1). One of the most productive of the world's oil plants, *E. guineensis* can live for up to 200 years, yielding two crops of fruit annually during its reproductive years.

Pendulous clusters of up to 700 plum-sized fruits teeter at the top of mature oil palm trees, which can grow to 65 feet above ground. Harvesting and milling palm fruit and kernels is tremendously labor intensive. The deftness and daring demonstrated by traditional palm fruit cutters is impressive. Once cut, there are two types of oil extracted from the palm fruit that partially account for its dual role as a food and as an industrial oil. From the fleshy outer pericarp comes the familiar bright orange culinary oil, which, at a cool room temperature, has a consistency of fresh milk pudding. And, from the cocooned inner seed comes palm-kernel oil, a "soft," highly processed, colorless, translucent oil developed to meet Europe's (chiefly Britain's) demand for tin cans, cheap margarine, and cheap soap (Billows and Beckwith 1892:3). Soft palm oil, low in free fatty acids, was perfect in consistency and price for machine lubrication, particularly tin-plate processing.

There are traditional, artisanal African methods of milling culinary palm oil from which Europeans' accelerated production systems were derived, but palm-kernel oil was thoroughly a function of European and British industry (Reader 1961:24). Regardless of processing style, timeliness was key. Once cut, palm fruit rapidly ferments. Cut bunches were quickly collected from fields and delivered to a mill where the fruit was "sterilized" and the pulp separated from the kernels. Kernels were bagged for transport and later processing. The pulp went through various extraction methods until an acceptable grade of culinary or lubricating oil was obtained. The oil was then poured into locally made drums for an impending sea voyage.

All the time that it moonlighted as an industrial tool, palm oil remained an important source of beta-carotenes, vitamin E, and fat in the traditional West African diet. But its use was never limited to the culinary sphere: Africans have long processed palm oil for illumination (lantern fuel) and homeopathic ointments. Available in the wild well before domestication, the entire tree was a resource for building materials (roof thatching, brushes), and its milky sap was the source of palm wine, the beloved (and deplored) African hooch.

But oil is this plant's gem. Its unctuous nature has taken it from dinner plate in Conakry, Guinea, to tin plate in Liverpool, England, and grocery and canteen shelves the world over. While many of West Africa's fruits and vegetables have supplied global markets, the oil palm is distinguished by the multiple, consequential functions it has served. As a machine lubricant, it helped build the physical infrastructure of the nineteenth century's global food system: one that would go on to alter the earth in unprecedented and pernicious ways. Beyond that, as Martin Lynn describes it, there were few nineteenth-century households that did not receive the benefits of the oil palm plant: "...railway carriages greased by palm oil carried members of the British public on their journeys, factory machinery lubricated by palm oil employed them and produced the goods that made their economy 'the workshop of the world,' while tins manufactured with palm oil canned their food, and palm kernels fed the cattle that produced the milk they drank with their tea" (Lynn 2002:188).

This plant, so iconic, so ubiquitous in West Africa's landscape, is both a food and an industrial ingredient used in transporting other foods. With its sunset palette of oranges, reds, and yellows and what some call a soft aroma of violets or plum cake, palm oil's place in West African cuisine dates back some 5,000 to 6,000 years, with oil palm fossil pollen identified in Miocene layers in the Niger Delta and archeological evidence of an oil palm trade among third-millennium Egyptians (Andah 1993:87). So essential to the West African diet and identity, palm oil was the oil chosen to provision transatlantic slave ships (Lynn 2002:2).

Let's return to my grandfather's shop. After that glass or two of rum, and a bit of camaraderie, Grandpère Michel would return home to his sleeping children and an oil lamp lighting the dining table. His wife, my Grandmère Jeanne, would assemble a plate: perhaps a heaping of warmed rice cradling a large piece of fish from the morning's catch that had stewed gently in a broth of palm oil, onions, tomatoes and hot peppers, finished with generous splashes of Maggi, imported from the shop. As a little indulgence, since he was on the road quite a bit, the house cook might freshly peel and slice a blackened plantain, perfectly ripe and sweet, and slip the thick rounds into blistering hot, red palm oil until the sides were crisp and caramelized.

After a good night's rest, Grandpère Michel would rise early, before the sounds of 11 children clanking about the breakfast table and scurrying off to school. He had to make his way to the Port of Conakry to inspect the arriving *outre-mer* shipments and his own departing cargo to the industries of France and England. But first, he would punch open a can of evaporated milk, pour it into his coffee, and butter a fresh baguette. Standing by the window, he would take his breakfast and look out onto the rising sun that drenched the palm fronds in a silvery hue. ∎

MAKALÉ FABER CULLEN *is the Creative Director of Wilderness of Wish (wildernessofwish.net), an ethnographic research and design practice based in New York City and operating internationally. She meets her family coming and going across three continents.*

REFERENCES

Andah, B. W. 1993. "Identifying Early Farming Traditions of West Africa." In *The Archaeology of Africa: Foods, Metals, and Towns*, edited by T. Shaw, P. Sinclair, B. Andah, and A. Okpoko, 240-254. London: Routledge.

H.C.. Billows, and H. Beckwith. 1892. "Palm Oil and Kernels, 3: 'Lagos Palm Oil." *Kew Bulletin of Miscellaneous Information* 69:200-8.

Bonin, Hubert. 2008. *CFAO (1887-2007): La reinvention permanente d'une entreprise de commerce outre-mer.* Paris: SFHOM.

Bonin, Hubert. 2001. "Des négociants français à l'assaut des places fortes commerciales britanniques: CFAO et SCOA en Afrique occidentale anglaise puis anglophone." In *Négoce blanc en Afrique noire. Le commerce de longue distance en Afrique subsaharienne du xviii au xx siècles*, edited by H. Bonin and Michel Cahen, 147-169. Paris: Société Française d'Histoire d'Outre-Mer,

Compagnie française de l'Afrique Occidentale (CFAO). 1900. *Afrique Occidental: notice de la Compagnie française de L'Afrique Occidentale.* Paris, Levallois-Perret.

Dunbar, Donald Earl. 1915. *The Tin-plate Industry: A Comparative Study of its Growth in the United States and in Wales.* Boston: Houghton Mifflin.

Dyke, K.O. 1956. *Trade and Politics in the Niger Delta, 1830-1885.* Oxford, UK: Oxford University Press.

Lynn, Martin. 2002. *Commerce and Economic Change in West Africa: The Palm Oil Trade in the Nineteenth Century.* Cambridge, UK: Cambridge University Press.

Milligan, Frank Marshall. 1914. *The Cultivation of the Oil Palm.* London: Crosby.

Oliver, Roland Anthony. 1991. *The African Experience.* London: Weidenfield & Nicolson.

Reader, W. J. 1961. *Unilever Plantations.* London: Unilever Limited.

DRAWINGS BY CHARLES KEEPING. FROM WILLIAM JOSEPH READER'S *UNILEVER PLANTATIONS* LONDON, UNILEVER LIMITED, (1961).

Nutrition Facts

8 servings per container

Serving size   2/3 cup (55g)

Amount per 2/3 cup

Calories   230

% DV*	
12%	**Total Fat** 8g
5%	Saturated Fat 1g
	Trans Fat 0g
0%	**Cholesterol** 0mg
7%	**Sodium** 160mg
12%	**Total Carbs** 37g
14%	Dietary Fiber 4g
	Sugars 1g
	Added Sugars 0g
	Protein 3g
10%	**Vitamin D** 2mcg
20%	**Calcium** 260mg
45%	**Iron** 8mg
5%	**Potassium** 235mg

* Footnote on Daily Values (DV) and calories reference to be inserted here.

Labels for Life

The labels on our food exist in a complex political struggle over consumers' attention. XAQ FROHLICH walks us through the information infrastructure of the label and its impact on our "choices."

STROLLING DOWN THE GROCERY STORE AISLE, THE CONSUMER IS awash in a sea of product information. Boxes, bags, and cans made of cardboard, plastic, or metal (with paper label wrap) are stained with a rainbow of color, intended to grab the attention of the passers-by; friendly, stately, or even slick company logos neatly frame bold, two-inch-tall letters spelling out in a commanding—though hopefully familiar—voice the brand of the food product. Littered across the "Principal Display Panel," to use the US Food and Drug Administration's (FDA) lexicon for the front of a package, are colorful (implied) health claims about the food's appealing qualities—"All Natural," "ORGANIC," "100% REAL," or "Clinically PROVEN to Help Reduce Cholesterol,"—which sit alongside more conventional marketplace puffery: "ORIGINAL" or "AMERICA'S FAVORITE." Along the side or back, there is an extended zone of food information: summaries of the company's romanticized history, instructions on how to prepare the food, further recipes that use it as an ingredient, or strategies to incorporate the product into a daily balanced diet.

It is here that the consumer discovers the conspicuously inconspicuous information panel, a black box modestly titled (in bolded, flat two-dimensional lettering and easy-to-read Helvetica) "Nutrition Facts."[1] Strikingly austere in its white-on-black eighth-grade-math-chart display format and ninth-grade-health-101 vocabulary, the Nutrition Facts panel almost leaps out at the consumer by its contrast with the more colorful, flamboyant product information displayed elsewhere on the package.

Over the course of the twentieth century, regulators, advertisers, public health advocates, doctors, scientists, and food manufactures have together created an "information infrastructure" that attempts to give information consistency and meaning. Labels are a technology of trust, not a simple source of competence: rather than a one-dimensional "everything is information" approach, it makes more sense to understand them as engaging a hierarchy of values shaped by public and private work that reflects changing understandings of governance, regulation, and individual responsibility.

Studies on improving labels usually look at whether people read them correctly; they focus on either comprehension

(is the information legible to the reader?) or priorities (does/should the information on the label matter to the reader?). But this focus on the individual misses the more dynamic marketplace for food labeling where normative and descriptive claims blur, where information has an aesthetic value and attention is the prime commodity, and where there is an interplay between the freedom of "commercial speech" (buyer beware!) and the legal, physical, and above all linguistic constraints of what one can meaningfully convey in so few words about a food. Thinking about labels as infrastructure leads us to different questions: how do changes in labels restructure the marketplaces in which they are embedded? How do they change food *itself*?

The FDA's "Nutrition Facts" panel, introduced in the 1970s and revised in the 1990s, is a good example of how regulators and businesses use labels to shape what Richard Thaler and Cass Sunstein so provocatively—and for my purposes conveniently—call the "choice architecture" of informational markets (2008). The FDA Nutrition Facts panel represents a more fundamental change in the regulation and structuring of food markets than simply helping consumers make health choices.

The introduction of the Nutrition Facts panel emerged from a half-century debate over how to rationalize food markets through product classification, including how foods would be distinguished from drugs or medicines.

TREATING OR EATING?
In the twentieth century, food labels and packaging rules were a key tactic in assuring product safety and quality in the market, forming an "architecture of authority" (Silbey and Ewing 2003). Two forms of authority were relevant: the FDA's interest in using labels as a tool for market accountability, and physicians' associations' concern with consolidating doctors' authority on matters of health. The 1938 Food, Drug and Cosmetic Act had given the FDA authority to seize or ban mislabeled products, but left ambiguous where the label—and the possible misinformation on it—started and stopped. The FDA could take action based on what was stated on the "label," the food law term for the physical label attached to food packaging, but over the course of the 1940s and 1950s a series of court cases extended FDA authority by expanding the legal term "labeling" to any and all informational materials that reference the label and/or bear upon its interpretation. Food labeling would therefore include advertising campaigns or health claims that might not appear directly on the food

---

1 The consumer might have been graciously directed to the nutrition panel by General Mills' Goodness Corner™ symbols, or by the "see back for details" notice accompanying Principal Display Panel health claims.

package, and even informational health pamphlets (though not books) that might be sold along with a dietary supplement. The product label thus sits at the center of a legally constructed terrain of intertextual or hypertextual references.

One of the FDA's main goals was the removal of ineffective or harmful products marketed as drugs or having drug-like powers. The 1938 Act passed as a result of public outrage over deaths caused by an adulterated drug product, Elixir Sulfanilamide, and one of the FDA's most common uses of the new law was to remove misbranded "food" products that made or implied health claims. For instance, FDA regulators developed the "jelly bean rule," which prohibited the sale of any candy-like product that included vitamins to promote a medical product to a popular market. One consequence of this system was that the FDA restricted the amount of information that would appear on food labels, limiting the labels to a standard identity, whereas drug labels or "special dietary foods" might have extensive ingredient panels or instructional information.

A key partner in the FDA's efforts was the American Medical Association (AMA), which had long been concerned with medical quackery and patent drugs. In the 1960s, the AMA worked with the FDA to develop a clearer prescription drug system with more detailed drug informational labeling, intended to aid and standardize physician practice. Raising the standards of quality in drug markets went hand in hand with campaigns to discredit alternative markets as medical and nutritional quackery. The AMA and FDA together would launch the "Campaign Against Nutrition Quackery" in the late 1950s and early 1960s to combat what one FDA Commissioner called "the nutritional 'big lie'—that the American food supply is impoverished and nutritionally deficient" (Larrick 1961).

"Food or drug," for the FDA and AMA, was not simply a decision about labeling, but about where that product would appear in the marketplace and who could sell it. Borderline products created headaches for regulators because they might appear at the drugstore, targeted to patients under counsel of a physician, but they also might appear in supermarkets next to the ordinary equivalent product. The introduction of Sweet'N Low, for example, brought artificial sweeteners to a whole new demographic of consumers because of its packaging in a sachet rather than pill or tablet, suggesting that it could be used not only as a supplement but also as a food additive. Under this regulatory regime, the AMA and FDA imagined a world where healthy individuals didn't need special information and could purchase food labeled as food, whereas patients could seek advice on health directly from doctors.

Despite the FDA and AMA's campaigns against nutrition and medical "quackery" and attempts to articulate clear rules separating special medical products from ordinary foods, people continued to buy special dietary products from alternative health markets, and advertisers continued to skirt the line between food and drugs when marketing health information about non-medical foods. By the early 1960s, the FDA was overwhelmed by the popular consumption of artificially sweetened sodas, concern over the "cholesterol scare," interest in low-fat diets, and the continued rise in vitamin-enriched foods and supplements. During this period one can find an odd alignment of right- and left-wing antiestablishment critiques of the FDA's food-drug labeling system as an intrusion by the government into personal choices. California Governor Ronald Reagan cited proposed FDA dietary regulations in 1968 as yet another example of how the FDA was destroying the freedom of industry to run its own affairs. "If I feel better taking a little vitamin C to ward off a cold," Reagan declared, "government can keep its sticky labels off my pill bottles" (*Food Chemical News* 1968:34). Michael Jacobson, founder of the Center for Science in the Public Interest, would write in 1972 about the problematic existence of what he called "silent labels" that "list none or only a few of the ingredients and additives that the food contains" (Jacobson 1972). The widely celebrated mantra of the consumer's "right to know," drawn from Kennedy's consumer's "bill of rights" at the start of the decade, was taken up on both sides to push for informational labeling. The informed consumer was no longer imagined as sick or healthy, but as moving within a continuum of healthfulness (Dumit 2012). Nutrition labeling now placed the responsibility for health on informed, active consumers managing their own lifestyles.

FROM SAFETY TO RESPONSIBILITY

In 1973, the FDA introduced new rules that dramatically changed its food labeling policies. It required a "nutrition information" label on any foods that made an explicit or implied health claim, and it chose to allow more vitamin-enrichment of ordinary foods without necessarily classifying them as special dietary foods. These changes allowed the industry to innovate and experiment without relying on the agency to endorse the results by setting standards. More significant, for the FDA, the change meant that it would now be regulating nutrient and ingredient information profiles as much or more than the standards for foods themselves.

As a result, in the 1970s there was an explosion of new diet foods labeled low in saturated fats or sodium, but also an explosion of explicit and implied health claims not officially permitted under the new system. A high-ranking government official, speaking of this period, would declare, "The grocery store has become the tower of Babel, and consumers need to be linguists, scientists, and mind readers to understand many of the labels they see" (Lyons & Rumore 1993: 249). Kellogg's All-Bran cereal was a prime example of these changes: it carried a statement, endorsed by the National Institutes of Health's (NIH) National Cancer Institute, that fiber had health properties shown to be associated with a reduction in incidences of colon cancer. Because Kellogg's got the NIH's permission, the FDA's hands were tied on declaring the product misbranded. Companies facing prosecution quickly used the All-Bran case as precedent for allowing their own disease claims. The National Cancer Institute campaign illustrates the growing popularity of public-private collaborations at this time, but it also illustrates the value of labels as a private-public infrastructure. The NIH was as eager as Kellogg's to get its campaign message onto the cereal box because doing so would spread its public health message well beyond the Institute's more conventional educational reach.

In the early 1990s the FDA overhauled the nutrition label, introducing the current "Nutrition Facts" panel. This label had several new features, including the percentage of recommended daily values, the calibration of amounts to standard serving sizes, and an average diet set at 2,000 calories a day. Now all foods, not just diet foods, would carry the label. Also important, however, was how the label fit into an entire infrastructure of health information. Any health claim or statement on a food on the front panel would have to direct readers to the label on the side or back panel. The idea was that this would help solve the problems with the food-drug divide by centralizing the flow of diet information in the market, situating the FDA as the main arbiter of what was sound scientific advice on diet and nutrition.

However, industry lobbyists now criticized the FDA label as an infringement on "freedom of commercial speech," echoing Reagan's criticisms two decades before. One representative of the industry lobbyist group Council for Responsible Nutrition stated its concern in a 1993 television interview:

...the FDA has a very narrow interpretation of the information they believe can be allowed to consumers. We believe that the Congress's intent [in the 1990 Nutrition Labeling and Education Act] was that there should be a free flow of information to allow consumers to know what the value of the product was. FDA has taken several years now, and it's literally choked off the flow of information to consumers, and we think that needs to be opened up (Taylor and Cordaro 1993).

Faced with these criticisms, FDA Commissioner David Kessler hedged his characterization of the label as liberating the consumer but containing apolitical information. In a 1994 television interview with Larry King, Kessler repeated the FDA line that "It's information for consumers [but] it's up to people what they do with it," to which King responded: "You'd have to be whack to be mad at information" (Kessler 1994). The new politics of nutrition labeling was no longer framed around healthy or sick, or "authentic" versus novel, but around whose responsibility it would be to sift through the information overload in the supermarket: big institutions or the individual? In the words of a CBS news report on the Nutrition Facts panel: "The new food label is designed to make experts out of everyone."

IS THE MEDIUM THE MESSAGE?

The focus on personal choice misses how some choices in "choice architecture" happen before the end consumer receives it. Nutrition labeling changed not only the information available about food, but the foods themselves. It resulted in a market restructuring away from standards of "food *qua* food" to food as information and components (ingredients and nutrients), which led companies to reformulate their food recipes to create better nutritional or ingredient profiles. This change in the food precedes the consumer-reader at the supermarket, yet directly affects what is eaten; it is an example of how mass foods are regularly redesigned within this information infrastructure.

Infrastructure is often a solution to problems of scale, where official standards are designed to coordinate complicated, heterogeneous markets. Infrastructure like the Nutrition Facts label is designed to be optimal for mass markets. Small changes on the label can work across big markets. This was why the FDA built its regulatory authority around the legal apparatus of "labeling" and surveilling informational, virtual markets rather than direct product seizures and bans. It also means that the message of nutrition labeling is not personal, but rather acts at a collective level, often with synergistic, nonlinear effects. Burkey Belser, the president of the firm hired to design the 1990s Nutrition Facts panel, noted, "Something that you see over and over and over and over again, across all media or all packaging and the like, gradually... seeps itself into the mind so that you start to...understand it and absorb it in ways that supersede reading" (Belser, personal communication, October 14, 2009). When infrastructure functions well, it is discreet and invisible; this can make it even more powerful in shaping behaviors. Very few actually read the Nutrition Facts label anymore, and yet most regularly talk about and think about food's nutrients. Indeed, one does not need to read—or even think—about the label for it to play a part in his or her everyday life. ■

XAQ FROHLICH *teaches in Valencia and researches the science of risk assessment and risk communication, food as a liminal object that bridges the environment and human health, and socially responsible consumption.*

REFERENCES

Dumit, Joseph. 2012. *Drugs for Life: How Pharmaceutical Companies Define Our Health*. Durham, NC: Duke University Press.

Food Chemical News. 1968. "FDA Says New Drug Clearance May Be Necessary for High-Level Vitamins." June 24, p. 34.

Jacobson, M. F. 1972. *Eater's Digest: The Consumer's Fact-Book of Food Additives*. New York: Doubleday.

Kessler, David. 1994. "Food Label Launch" [videorecording]. *CNN Larry King Live*. VHS tape at National Library of Medicine.

Larrick, George P. 1961. "Report on Quackery from the FDA." Delivered to the AMA/FDA National Congress on Medical Quackery, October 6.

Lyons, Jean, and Martha Rumore. 1993. "Food Labeling Then and Now." *Journal of Pharmacy & Law* 171(2).

Silbey, Susan S., and Patricia Ewick. 2003. "The Architecture of Authority: The Place of Law in the Space of Science." In *The Place of Law*, edited by Austin Sarat, Lawrence Douglas, and Martha Umphrey, 77-108. Ann Arbor: University of Michigan Press.

Taylor, Mike, and J. B. Cordaro. 1993. "Michael Taylor of FDA, et al." [videorecording]. *Fox Morning News*. VHS tape at National Library of Medicine.

Thaler, Richard H., and Cass R. Sunstein. 2008. *Nudge: Improving Decisions about Health, Wealth, and Happiness*. New Haven, CT: Yale University Press.

Iconoclasm
in the
Supermarket

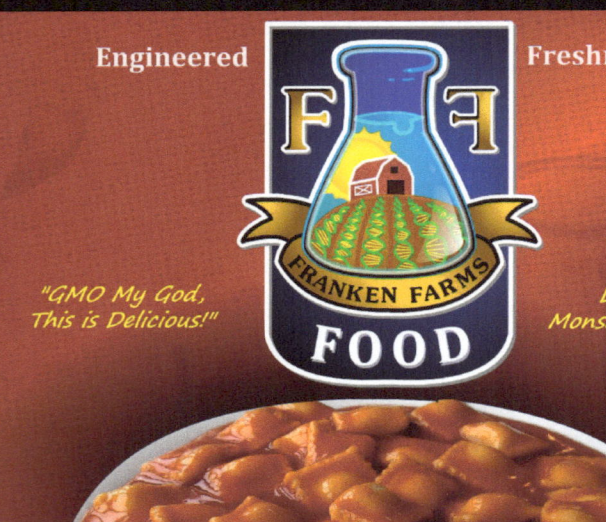

Engineered **Freshness!**

"GMO My God, This is Delicious!"

FRANKEN FARMS
FOOD

Lab Tested, Monsanto Approved!

Franken Farms Labs GMO Awareness Project

March Against
Monsanto
Serving Size 100 g   (Wordwide March)

Find a Location Near You

Calendar	May 25 2013
	% Daily Value*
Raise Awareness 1g	7%
Protect Our Food 7mg	10%
Support 22mg	2%
Local Farmers 13mg	1.5%
Organic Solutions 9mg	20%
Demand 8g	18%
Accountability 5g	9%
Protest 31g	

www.Occupy-Monsanto.com
fb.com/MarchAgainstMonsanto

* Stand against Genetically Modified Food. Join your city in a March Against Monsanto.

0 70183 50055

Monsanto

INGREDIENTS: United States (Washington DC, New York City, Miami, Phoenix, San Francisco, Chicago, Boston, Los Angeles, Atlanta, St. Louis, Las Vegas, Orlando, New Orleans, St. Paul/Minneapolis, Milwaukee), Canada (Montreal, Toronto, Vancouver), Europe (London, Paris, Athens, Amsterdam, Rome, Madrid, Stockholm, Barcelona), Australia, New Zealand, Belgium, Ecuador, Chile, Mexico, Israel, South Africa, India, and many more locations worldwide.

March-Against-Monsanto.com

What's in YOUR food?
facebook.com/FrankenFarmsLabs

Engineered **Freshness!**

"GMO My God, This is Delicious!"

FRANKEN FARMS
FOOD

Lab Tested, Monsanto Approved!

Franken Farms Labs GMO Awareness Project

March Against
Monsanto
Serving Size 100 g   (Wordwide March)

Find a Location Near You

Calendar	May 25 2013
	% Daily Value*
Raise Awareness 1g	7%
Protect Our Food 7mg	10%
Support 22mg	2%
Local Farmers 13mg	1.5%
Organic Solutions 9mg	20%
Demand 8g	18%
Accountability 5g	9%
Protest 31g	

www.Occupy-Monsanto.com
fb.com/MarchAgainstMonsanto

* Stand against Genetically Modified Food. Join your city in a March Against Monsanto.

0 70183 50055

Monsanto

INGREDIENTS: United States (Washington DC, New York City, Miami, Phoenix, San Francisco, Chicago, Boston, Los Angeles, Atlanta, St. Louis, Las Vegas, Orlando, New Orleans, St. Paul/Minneapolis, Milwaukee), Canada (Montreal, Toronto, Vancouver), Europe (London, Paris, Athens, Amsterdam, Rome, Madrid, Stockholm, Barcelona), Australia, New Zealand, Belgium, Ecuador, Chile, Mexico, Israel, South Africa, India, and many more locations worldwide.

March-Against-Monsanto.com

What's in YOUR food?
facebook.com/FrankenFarmsLabs

What happens when activists re-label your food? **Javier Lezaun** explores the "Label It Yourself" movement and its ambivalent power.

"Label It Yourself!" In the last decade, this slogan has mobilized different strands of dissatisfaction with the way food products are identified and their qualities made known (or, more often, unknown) to consumers. Instead of waiting for companies and governments to provide truthful representations of foods and their ingredients, citizens are encouraged to "take things into their own hands," append new labels to products, and bring to the surface attributes hidden or misrepresented in the standard container.

Like other forms of graffiti, writing on food packages introduces in the ostensibly public but highly controlled environment of the supermarket a surreptitious, clandestine channel of communication between consumers. The food product becomes a vehicle for delivering unsanctioned messages, and the act of perusing the supermarket shelves suddenly acquires a new, suspenseful quality. This sort of informational intrusion cuts, however, both ways: by adding their own interpretations to food packages, consumers interfere with the marketing strategies of food companies, but they also upend efforts to regulate the food system through the official certification of product qualities. The result is a proliferation of writing that makes the market an even more cacophonous and bewildering space than it already is.

Label It Yourself (LIY) activism is often a subterranean affair: most acts of food relabeling go unreported, and to the extent a coherent LIY movement exists, it is made up of decentralized and only loosely coordinated campaigns at the margins of mainstream food reform movements. Yet guerrilla labeling is widespread enough to have prompted the food industry to lobby for its criminalization. In the United States, the Product Packaging Protection Act of 2002 (S. 1223, Sec. 2) amended federal product-tampering legislation and made it a crime to add any writing to a food product prior to its purchase. "Whoever, without the consent of the manufacturer, retailer or distributor, intentionally tampers with a consumer product that is sold in interstate or foreign commerce by knowingly placing or inserting any writing in the consumer product, or in the container for the consumer product, before the sale of the consumer product to any consumer shall be fined under this title, imprisoned not more than 3 years, or both."

In the congressional hearings that preceded the Act, spokespersons for the food industry denounced a growing tendency to use food products to deliver illicit ("offensive") messages: pornographic drawings, racist literature, anti-meat brochures, and religious tracts were some of the examples cited before an audience of worried legislators. In the words of the Chief Marketing Counsel for Kraft Foods: "These incidents of tampering amount to product hijacking." Criminal penalties were necessary, he argued, "to prevent these product tamperers from commandeering a cereal box as their personal soap box."[1]

CURRENTLY, THE MOST VISIBLE LIY CAMPAIGN in the United States targets products thought to contain genetically modified organisms (GMOs). Spurred by the refusal of federal authorities to introduce the mandatory identification of genetically modified foods, and further motivated by the defeat of several popular pro-labeling initiatives (most recently Proposition 37 in California and Washington's Initiative 522), LIY activists have taken it upon themselves to manually tag (Menchini 2013) foods they suspect of containing genetically modified materials.

"Knowing what is in our food and where our food is coming from is our right," claims a LIY manifesto. "We will label GMOs, we will rescue words like All Natural, Natural Flavors from being hijacked, we will expose unfair practices. If there is nothing to hide then why hide it???!!!! Label It Yourself."

The movement's radical DIY approach sets it apart from other contemporary pro-labeling movements. The "Just Label It" campaign

---

1   The Product Packaging Protection Act: Keeping Offensive Material Out of Our Cereal Boxes: Hearing on S. 1233 Before the Subcommittee on Antitrust, Business Rights, and Competition of the Committee on the Judiciary, United States Senate. 107th Cong. (First Session, August 1, 2002). Serial No. J-107-35.

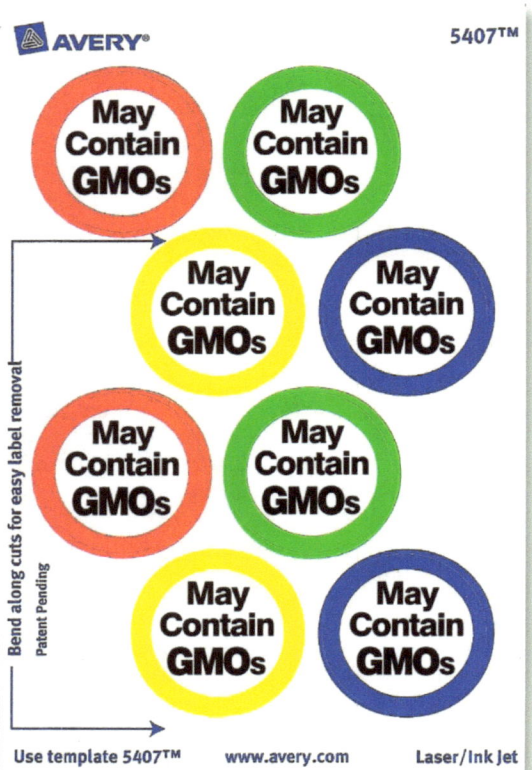

FIGURE 1. LIY sticker label template

two cornstalks for crossbones, the words "Warning May Contain GMOs," and a QRcode or URL directing the consumer to websites with additional information about genetically modified foods.

This iconography had the merit of highlighting the overt, illicit nature of the relabeling action—it is difficult to mistake the image for an official identifier, and here, as with street graffiti, evidence of trespassing gives the message a particular force—but it also generated a great deal of controversy. It put off sympathizers who would have preferred "more subtle" designs—"ie less SKULLS", in the words of a visitor to the LIY Facebook page—if only to lessen the chance that, if caught, they would be reported to the police or banned from shopping in the store again.

Indeed, many activists argue that LIY actions should minimize the defacement of the original package and fit as seamlessly as possible within the existing product layout. "I wanna see smaller labels that don't cover up the existing product info," a participant in the discussions points out, "if only to be less likely to be pulled by grocers. More subversive." When another visitor to the LIY Facebook page posted images of products labeled with a small, round, fluorescent sticker containing the words "Warning: may contain GMOs" in clean typeface and no additional image, the design was commended by many for its similarity to official, corporate imagery. "That looks like a real label put by the manufacturer! Well done!"

Over time, the "skull and cornstalks" iconography has given way to more aseptic labels. Currently the favored design is a white rectangle with the words "GENETICALLY ENGINEERED" in large type and no accompanying image. This evolution in label aesthetics towards a certain matter-of-factness has been accompanied by a disambiguation of the message: the noncommittal "may contain" of previous stickers has disappeared in favor of a more assertive declaration of the genetically modified nature of the product.

By dropping the qualifying "may contain," however, the new label elides a key and perennial point of contention in LIY forums: what sort of epistemic authority legitimizes the marking of a certain product as genetically engineered? How do we know (and to what extent do we need to know) whether a specific product does in fact contain GMOs?

This issue frequently comes up in discussions of products (or retailers) with a particularly green or wholesome image. "I support what you are doing," writes a visitor to the LIY Facebook page, "because I think this is a great way to use civil disobedience on a grass roots level to get the word out about GMOs, which people are entitled to know about. But PLEASE make sure people are reading before they label—someone put a label on a Silk carton, and not only are they Non-GMO Project certified, it also says: 'GMOs? No thanks!' on their cartons,

New 2" x 2" sticker templates with QR code available for download at www.labelityourself.org/liy
Great for labeling advertisements and GMO food signs!

FIGURE 2. Early LIY label template.

(http://justlabelit.org/), for instance, a coalition of several hundred nongovernmental organizations, concentrates its efforts on petitioning the US Food and Drug Administration and Congress in favor of the mandatory labelling of genetically modified foods, but refrains from asking its supporters to carry out the labeling themselves. In contrast, LIY presents itself as "a decentralized, autonomous grassroots campaign to empower people to make educated decisions about what is in their food, without waiting for government or corporations to do it for them." A handful of websites, Twitter feeds, and Facebook profiles[2] structure a collective debate on LIY tactics, and serve to disseminate labeling templates and photographic evidence of relabeling actions.

THE ISSUES THAT BEDEVIL LIY ACTIVISM and generate the most heated discussion in its online forums are those typical of movements that contest the power of official images: the interrelated questions of the aesthetics of defacement and the ultimate truth value of the iconoclastic gesture.

As the campaign took off in 2012, the most common label used in LIY actions featured a skull with

---

2   See http://labelityourself.tumblr.com/, https://twitter.com/labelityourself, and https://www.facebook.com/LabelitYourself.

FIGURE 3. New simplified LIY sticker design.

which goes a step further even than getting certified. Clearly, the person who did that has not educated themselves [sic] enough to be putting labels on things."

These complaints, and the counterarguments that follow, point to the conundrum at the heart of the LIY movement: how can a decentralized movement, predicated on the fact that food manufacturers are withholding relevant information about the origins and composition of their products, legitimize its own acts of identification? The same circumstances that recommend collective action—a situation of structural ignorance sanctioned by the passivity of regulators—are prone to throw the movement into divisive quarrels about the appropriateness of its targets. The dilemma is put succinctly by another visitor to the Facebook discussion, complaining about the (in her mind) unjust tagging of a certain retailer's products: "I agree that we need truth in labelling, but I'm not comfortable with vandalism."

Thus, while the "may contain" label struck many as too timid, at least it made room for a degree of uncertainty, or even unknowability, as to the exact nature of the product being tagged. In contrast, the unambiguous and emphatic "GENETICALLY ENGINEERED" would seem to speak with the same force (and font) as a corporate or state-sanction text, but it does so at the expense of eliding questions about the legibility of production systems and supply chains that were at the root of the movement to begin with.

"IN HISTORICAL TERMS," writes Boris Groys, "the iconoclastic gesture has never functioned as an expression of a skeptical attitude toward the truth of the image…. The desecration of ancient idols is performed only in the name of other, more recent gods." In his discussion of the artistic "martyrdom of the image", Groys notes how, "for the time being, commodity brands will remain our latest household gods, at least until some new, nascent iconoclastic anger rises up against them too" (Groys 2008:67–8).

The iconoclasm of the LIY movement is strikingly iconophilic. It operates by adding signifiers to a world of consumption already saturated by images, and thus partakes of the logic of advertising. LIY websites and forums are sometimes little

more than visual displays of relabeled products. In fact, the true rite of passage for a would-be activist is the sharing of photographs showing the results of LIY actions. Some go further, and use the marking of genetically modified foods as an opportunity to design and exhibit elaborate, often sarcastic, transgenic counter-iconographies.

Yet, it is possible to imagine an alternative version of LIY: a form of activism that would operate by subtracting, rather than adding, product identifiers. A movement that, instead of enriching the informational content of the package, would aim to emphasize its opacity, and in so doing reveal the radical inscrutability at the heart of food production and distribution systems.

Such iconophobic tactics would truly unleash the power of LIY activism, which lies in its ability to shatter pretensions of transparency by introducing a moment of surprise and suspicion in the encounter between product and consumer. Who put this label here? What does it mean? How should I act? This is of course an ambivalent power, and the reason why LIY is potentially so disruptive (and irritating) for governments, corporations, and consumers alike. For while it makes a visit to the supermarket a potentially more eventful affair than one would have expected, it also interrupts, at least for a brief moment, the trance-like modes of reading that underlie everyday acts of consumption. ■

JAVIER LEZAUN *is based at the Institute for Science, Innovation and Society, University of Oxford.*

REFERENCES

Groys, Boris. 2008. *Art Power.* Cambridge, MA: The MIT Press.

Menchini, Peter. 2013. "Got GMOs? Label It Yourself!" Vimeo video, January 3, 2013. http://vimeo.com/56731712.

ANTHROPOLOGIST AND RETAIL
CONSULTANT **MICHAEL POWELL** TAKES
US ON A STROLL DOWN AISLE #6. WHAT'S IN
THE CENTER OF THE GROCERY STORE AND WHY IS IT
CAUSING A CRISIS IN THE INDUSTRY?

All Lost in the Supermarket

PHOTO: MARK SARDELLA

I FIRST HEARD the "Aisle 6" joke while interviewing a grocery industry veteran: "Take a grocery store executive, blindfold him, and place him in Aisle 6 of any grocery store anywhere in the country," said the consultant. "Ask him to guess what chain he is in." Chances are, he can't. The "punchline" is left unsaid, because grocery insiders intuitively know the problem: nearly every grocery store's Aisle 6 looks exactly the same.

Consider the "center store," the long aisle after aisle of "Aisle 6s," stocked mostly with packaged goods. These are the aisles that make the grocery shopping experience such a loathsome chore for so many people, and a crisis for supermarket executives and grocery story owners. As a cultural anthropologist who studies the supermarket industry through an ethnographic lens, I watch recent trends shaping the center store landscape. And as someone who works for a retail strategy and design firm—my "day job"—I work closely with top executive teams to understand their shoppers and consumers, the world of food, and the store experience, in order to help create prototype retail spaces. As both observer and expert, I

can see some curious discrepancies between the internal struggles of a unique and complex industry and the criticisms and projections of public audiences outside the industry.

Take, for instance, Rule 12 of Michael Pollan's *Food Rules*, which urges readers to steer clear of the center store:

Rule #12: Shop the peripheries of the supermarket and stay out of the middle.
Most supermarkets are laid out the same way: Processed food products dominate the center aisles of the store, while the cases of mostly fresh food—produce, meat and fish, dairy—line the walls. If you keep to the edges of the store you'll be much more likely to wind up with real food in your shopping cart. This strategy is not foolproof, however, since things like high fructose corn syrup have crept into the dairy case under the cover of flavored yogurts and the like
(Pollan 2009:27).

Pollan is not alone in this critique, but there is another critical voice focused on the center store: the industry itself. From the industry's perspective, something is not quite right with the center store, but the problem is not health, the obesity epidemic, or where our food comes from, nor a conspiratorial story of how major corporations collude to manipulate the American stomach. It is a story about the slow-paced evolution of a $600 billion food retail industry, with 3.4 million employees in America. But if the center store represents a quandary, the industry's solution cannot be, as Pollan might hope, to simply get rid of it. The center store will be an inevitable component of the industry's transformation.

A BRIEF HISTORY OF THE CENTER STORE

In the early twentieth century, American shoppers experienced a very different supermarket. Compared to the 50,000 square feet of average stores today, the first supermarkets measured roughly 5,000 to 10,000 square

feet. And while the contemporary supermarket experience typically begins in the produce department today, where grocers seek to invoke a perception of "freshness," some early supermarkets lacked a produce department altogether. Nor did many of these early supermarkets have a bakery department, meat department, or dairy department. The grocery store was not initially intended to be the only food-shopping destination, but one that supplemented trips to the butcher, the baker, the greengrocer, or the dairy (Mayo 1993).

The genesis and thrust of the early supermarket store format was the center store. A handful of aisles stocked with packaged goods, cans, and barrels of shelf-stable staples, center store products made a direct connection to the average American family's pantry (compare with Cochoy, this issue). Because these early stores did not focus on fresh products, the business model was closely tied to the rise of massive consumer packaged goods (CPG) companies through the course of the twentieth century such as Procter & Gamble and Kellogg's. The center store was and continues to be a central medium for the

CPG industry, which has played a primary role in shaping and influencing its size and form.

Over time, separated specialty shops, such as the butcher, were integrated into the supermarket, evolving from minor store amenities into entire departments that populated the "perimeter" of the store experience. This fueled growth throughout the industry, but the center store continued to be the supermarket's central economic engine.

Today, industry insiders argue, the fortunes of the center store have tumbled. As a percentage of overall sales growth for the industry, the center store lags behind perimeter departments, such as prepared foods, produce, bakery, and meat. Why? Competing expert positions on the answer offer a glimpse into the evolution of the center store.

REINVENTING THE AISLE

Recent supermarket studies reveal fewer shoppers pushing carts up and down center store aisles. Shoppers spend less time in center store and make fewer purchasing decisions there, opting to pace quickly rather than linger. Observers, including store-level managers and supermarket employees, note increasing numbers of shoppers pushing their carts along the edges of the center store, pausing at the edge of each aisle to peer down. Without much to pique their interest, and amid a cacophony of packages and signs, all screaming out for their attention, more people shop these aisles in a highly tactical manner.

The industry journal *Supermarket News* explored the findings and recommendations of a recent study conducted by VideoMining, a shopper marketing "intelligence" firm (Alaimo 2013). Using cameras positioned on the ceilings of stores across the country, VideoMining monitored shopping behaviors in the frozen department and found that "[f]or every 100 people who enter a supermarket, 38 visit the frozen aisle, with 22 actively engaging with product and 16 just passing through without stopping.... Of the 22 who stop, 17 convert into buyers, while five leave without buying, which [Rajeev Sharma, Chief Executive Officer of VideoMining] describes as 'leakage.'"

VideoMining recommends grocery stores prevent leakage by "improving space navigation" and "navigational assistance," or, in other words, by altering the "planogram" level (the visual schematic maps that guide store teams in placing products on the shelf; these planograms have traditionally been controlled by each category's best-selling CPG company). For VideoMining, as well as many in the CPG industry, refined planograms are the magical solution that can attract more shoppers into center store.

Beyond shelf-level solutions, store chains, consultants, and CPGs are experimenting with the actual context or shape of the center store. Aside from some experimental store layout formats that have mostly failed, most of these innovations focus on a single aisle or category in the center store. For example, one major CPG recently experimented with the cookies and crackers aisle in a small number of midwestern grocery stores. They removed more than a dozen feet of shelving, included a small open refrigerated case with milk, and incorporated a wooden kitchen table merchandised with products, recipe cards, and other evocative objects. Although the project was successful on many levels—increasing shopping time, customer satisfaction, and sales for the entire category—the roll-out of this innovation by the CPG company demonstrated the difficulties of making substantial changes: CPG companies and grocery stores were upset with the loss of product space, stores complained about the operational complexity of stocking milk in the center store, and no one could agree on who would pay for the roll-out. In the end, the experiment ended with a redesign into a wood veneer endcap that was much cheaper to produce and exactly replicated the existing center store aisle configuration.

All of these experiments and innovations ultimately focus on the "tactical" rather than the "strategic" level. Reinventing the aisle, revising planograms, and reworking the store's environmental context all require different operational arrangements, but none of these tactical innovations fundamentally alters the business model of the supermarket. Facing a crisis, these experiments represent an earnest, but likely misguided, hope that no major reevaluation of the grocery store chassis is necessary.

LOSING ON PRICE, WINNING ON QUALITY

CPG revenues continue to rise on an annual basis, but where are shoppers going to get the everyday staples of the American household if not the supermarket center store? The crux of this problem likely has less to do with the flow of shopping behaviors in the center store and more to do with the products and their retailers.

Grocery store executives around the country recite the critique by heart; paraphrased, it goes, "A can of corn is a can of corn. Center store is not a place where we can differentiate our business." Shoppers care about where a cucumber came from and the qualities of how it smells, feels, looks, and tastes. But the qualities of center store products have been engineered to create a degree of consistency and reliability indifferent to the retailer. The competitive battle inside the center store is about cost and price, because the center store is fully commoditized by the shopper. Ironically enough, this is exactly the shopping behavior grocery stores had earlier encouraged to win over so many shoppers from the "mom and pop" grocers and smaller independent supermarket chains.

Although farms, CPGs, wholesalers, and store chains have long viewed food products as commodities to be sold, stored, processed, and shipped, when shoppers purchase them, they are transformed from a price-focused commodity object into a multilayered meaningful object, process, or behavior. This relationship, which Daniel Miller (1998) compares to an act of ritual sacrifice, is at the core of the center store crisis: a crisis of price and quality.

Walmart, Costco, WinCo, and other big-box retailers have become "category killers," strategically grabbing supermarkets' center store revenues by focusing almost solely on low prices. Walmart began selling groceries only in the mid-1990s, but today they enjoy the largest market share of grocery sales in the United States. They accomplished this remarkable rise by focusing on an "Everyday Low Price" (EDLP) strategy, which has been especially effective in traditional center store categories. Walmart and others own what people in the industry call a "price perception" reputation: shoppers believe Walmart products cost less than the grocery store, even when this is not always the case. Most grocery store industry veterans I have spoken with find Walmart's price perception infuriating. Having grown up in an era when their stores won the price perception battles, these veterans have relented the battle against Walmart only in the past decade. Even if they can beat Walmart on price, they now know they cannot win the perception campaign.

Conversely, a different approach to the center store is summed up in optimistic articles like this one from *Supermarket News*: "Survey: Consumers Value Quality Over Low Prices" (2012). For grocery store executives, quality is the way to beat their low-price competitors. Grocery insiders generally agree that while price-focused competitors such as Walmart win on price perception, they lose at quality perception: shoppers simply don't believe the quality of the Walmart perimeter departments is as good as those at the supermarket.

PRIVATE LABELS AND THE HOLY GRAIL

The focus on quality leads to a different strategy—a holy grail, of sorts, that only a few darlings of the industry have attained—to provide a *whole-store* experience that decisively "wins" on quality perception, without losing the center store price war.

In this respect, no traditional grocery store brand is more revered inside the industry than Wegmans, a relatively small but highly profitable chain with more than 80 stores throughout the mid-Atlantic region (see, for example, Gallagher 2013). Wegmans departs from a conventional grocery store format with an additional avenue on one side of the store to combine the best of the traditional grocery store with the indulgent offerings of more specialized gourmet food retailers. But Wegmans' success is not only due to increased revenues in their gourmet avenue: having built a quality reputation in perimeter departments, Wegmans has used its reputation equity to build a "private label" brand that reinvigorates the center store.

Private label, or "generic," center store products have long had a bad reputation. In the past, they often looked like government-issue food rations, more suitable for nuclear fallout shelters and homeless encampments than the dinner table. Wegmans and others figured out how to dramatically elevate the quality of private label products and, by pivoting off price points set by national CPG competitors, sell products of comparable quality for lower prices. Industry trade magazines and even national media point to the "Great Recession" of the late 2000s as a key moment in the evolution of private labels, as shoppers

a series of "price freezes" on everyday staple products in the center store that are applicable only to Wegmans private label products (Freeman 2013).

Some alternative-format grocery stores, such as Trader Joe's, have unreservedly invested in the private label strategy. Trader Joe's stores carry just a fraction of the number of products that a regular grocery store does, and more than 90 percent of those products are private label. If there is one ketchup, it's going to be Trader Joe's ketchup: national CPG brands, like Heinz, are left out of the mix. In doing so, the brand's strategy is essentially focused on a kind of metacritique of the traditional supermarket center store and the CPG industry that played such a key role in its development. The mass acceptance of private label speaks to the increasing numbers of shoppers who are nominally aware of the critique.

NEW CRITICAL SHOPPING STRATEGIES

In the end, the material realities of store size, store format, chain size, long-term supplier relationships, and established business models make the center store crisis an enduring one: it's not going away anytime soon. But we might nonetheless imagine a near-future scenario where discerning "real food" from "processed food," as per Michael Pollan's critique, is no longer a simple task. In or out of the center store, new critical shopping strategies may be required. ■

MICHAEL POWELL *has a PhD in cultural anthropology from Rice University, and currently works in Los Angeles at the strategy and design firm Shook Kelley.*

were more willing to downgrade product brands before downgrading shopping destination brands (Martin 2008). They would rather choose the Wegmans private label brand over national competitors than shop elsewhere. Wegmans' private label share today is around 25 percent in the center store (Hofbauer 2013), while most in the industry average around 15 percent (Angrisani 2008).

At the same time, Wegmans keeps pounding on a price perception campaign. But instead of touting themselves as having the lowest prices around, their message is fairness. Several years ago, Wegmans president Danny Wegman created a series of commercials and videos about fair and consistent prices that explained the store's pricing strategy with charts and graphs to shoppers (Shope 2002). More recently, Wegmans has received media attention for

REFERENCES

Alaimo, Dan. 2013. "Fine-Tune Frozen Layouts for Big Sales Increases." *Supermarket News* December 19. http://supermarketnews.com/store-design-amp-construction/fine-tune-frozen-layouts-big-sales-increases.

Angrisani, Carol. "Private Label: Behind The Report." *Supermarket News* January 28. http://supermarketnews.com/center-store/private-label-behind-report.

Freeman, Chris. 2013. "Wegmans Extends Private Label Price Freeze." *Private Label Buyer* January 3. http://www.privatelabelbuyer.com/articles/87084-wegmans-extends-private-label-price-freeze.

Gallagher, Julie. "Wegmans Tops D.C.-Area Stores in Price, Quality." *Supermarket News* November 4. http://supermarketnews.com/shopper-insights/wegmans-tops-dc-area-stores-price-quality-video.

Hofbauer, Randy. 2013. "Wegmans: A Celebration Of Food." *Private Label Store Brands* January 1. http://www.plstorebrands.com/top-story-wegmans__a_celebration_of_food_-3922.html.

Martin, Andrew. 2008. "Store Brands Lift Grocers In Troubled Times." *New York Times* December 12. http://www.nytimes.com/2008/12/13/business/13private.html?pagewanted=all&_r=0.

Mayo, James M. 1993. *The American Grocery Store: The Business Evolution of an Architectural Space.* Westport, CT: Greenwood Press.

Miller, Daniel. 1998. *A Theory of Shopping.* Ithaca, NY: Cornell University Press.

Pollan, Michael. 2009. *Food Rules: An Eater's Manual.* New York: Penguin Books.

Supermarket News. 2012. "Survey: Consumers Value Quality Over Low Prices." *Supermarket News* September 28. http://supermarketnews.com/top-75-retailers-amp-wholesalers/survey-consumers-value-quality-over-low-prices.

Shope, Dan. 2002. "Wegmans President Stars In Video." *The Morning Call (Lehigh Valley)* April 2. http://articles.mcall.com/2002-04-07/business/3412844_1_danny-wegman-wegmans-food-markets-pricing.

Infrastructures of Credibility

What makes a claim believable? **Bart Penders** and **Steven Flipse** explore two cases of credibility engineering.

T he idea came from lorry drivers who regularly visited southern and eastern Europe. They were struck by the beauty of local women, and especially taken aback by their breast sizes. So the "Edric Original" breast growth pill was born, filled with *hop*, the apparent key dietary difference between large-chested southern and eastern European women and everyone else (Scholtens 1997). *The complete programme will set you back €540: a bargain.*[1]

What is it about this offer that makes us question its credibility? Why do we consider some claims as more credible than others? Which elements characterize the credible claim and what infrastructure supports the engineering of credibility for those who produce and sell food? Here, we briefly present two claims and trace how their credibility was established to illustrate the infrastructure hosting the labor and resources that build and maintain (or demolish) credibility. We restrict ourselves to a single sustainability claim and a single health claim, and refer to Flipse and Penders (2012) and Penders and Nelis (2011) for more detailed accounts.

We first discuss the claim that biological production of succinic acid is more sustainable than petrochemical production, and then move towards the claim that margarine fortified with phytosterols lowers cholesterol. While both exist in different realms, we will argue that they share a similar path through the "infrastructure of credibility."

CREDIBLY GREEN

The Dutch multinational life sciences and materials company Royal DSM N.V. develops a "greener," sustainable alternative for petrochemically produced succinic acid, which can be used as a food preservative or as a component in bioplastics. In contrast to the margarine example that follows, the users of DSM's products are not individual consumers, but companies who process these products into other products, ranging from foods to plastics. As such, the development of DSM's sustainability-related claims take place beyond the consumer's gaze. Sustainability claims are made legible through percentages of reduction of used resources or produced waste involved in the development of new products, using prospective product life cycle assessments (LCAS).

Sustainability is a self-identified priority for the company, based upon the requests and demands of its customers and its prominence in DSM's mission statement. DSM produces ingredients; if its customers use these ingredients to produce products marketed as "green" or "sustainable," they require or demand support for that claim. To that end, DSM studies the environmental footprint of its products, and mobilizes the results of those footprint studies in marketing claims, for the benefit of selling the product: succinic acid, in this case.

The main tool deployed to develop credible sustainability claims on greener products is the prospective LCA. It is an analysis meant to display quantitatively what will be the full impact of a production process on the environment. Simply put, this entails calculating every single step of the process into kilograms of carbon dioxide produced, capturing only ecological and environmental definitions of sustainability and leaving social and economic sustainability aside for the moment. The scientists involved present these numbers in literature and conferences, often in percentages of reduced carbon dioxide, liters of wastewater, and

1   See Erdic's website at http://www.erdic.nl/ (accessed November 18, 2013).

kilowatt-hours of energy. For the benefit of credibility, numbers are presented as transparently as possible, so everyone can check the calculations.

Making a prospective LCA is, however, easier said than done. When a novel production process is being developed, such as the biological production of succinic acid, its characteristics are not fully known. Pioneering such a new production process requires a high-quality LCA. However, for an LCA to be complete, details of that process are required. This presents DSM's scientists with four practical problems.

First, location determines the content of the LCA, and this location is still unknown upfront. Producing succinic acid in Brazil could mean using sugar cane, energy generated by water power, and a transport sector running on bioethanol. A location in China could mean using less energy-rich rice, energy from coal power, and transportation based on outdated diesel engines. Second, calculating carbon dioxide production is difficult: scientists don't know how much energy will be used, how much transportation will be required, and which raw material will be used. Working around these obstacles requires developing multiple scenarios, each with their own LCA. The way these scenarios are built and calculated, and the way these are perceived by higher-level management, determine the actual location of production and all the consequences of this choice. LCA, this way, is used to *produce credibility internal* to DSM, which is in line with the arguments of Freidberg (see this issue). LCAs thus compete with economic planning studies and scenarios for influence in business decisions. Those decisions, in turn, influence the selection of scenarios used in the LCAs.

Third, new problems arise when comparing the prospective LCAs of biological production with the current LCA of the petrochemical production of succinic acid. Petrochemical production has been around for half a century and has been optimized so much in that time that it is not always clear whether biological production processes can compete with those established methods. Scenarios exist in which the biological production route of succinic acid results can yield an inferior LCA compared with the petrochemical alternative. Thus, the fourth reason why making prospective LCAs is difficult arises: the rules for properly performing an LCA are not always clear. As a result, comparing LCAs performed by different companies or institutes is difficult and uninformative. Furthermore, where does the LCA of the ingredient end and that of the product begin? Does transport of the ingredient towards the customer belong to DSM's LCA or to the customer's LCA?

Ultimately, the LCA will be mobilized in

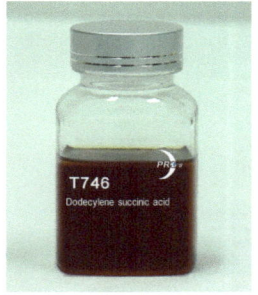

marketing. Some quantification of sustainability will be produced. However, because of these uncertainties, complexities, controversies, and disputes over what an LCA is or ought to be, that number will not automatically be credible inside the company or outside of it. In addition, the sustainability claim's origin matters: corporate claims tend to be judged critically. The credibility of DSM's LCAs needs support.

That support is offered in the form of an independent referee, judging and validating LCAs of all types. An example of a Dutch agency doing this type of work is the Copernicus Institute for Sustainable Development, connected to Utrecht University. This institute independently vetted DSM's prospective LCA calculations. In this particular case, their results were quite similar to DSM's, supporting the validity of DSM's own calculations.

By highlighting this similarity, not only does the quantification gain credibility, but the trustworthiness of the claimant also is supported. The independently verified and approved values are (partially) decoupled from their *interested* origins and *made legible and visible* to potential purchasers of DSM's ingredients through a marketing campaign focused on quantifiers and offering prospective purchasers draft versions of sustainability claims of their own. As a result, DSM performs a significant part of the credibility engineering for their customers' claims. They are selling food and bioplastic ingredients as well as marketing ingredients, and they come as a package deal.

CREDIBLY HEALTHY

The LCA is a desired marketing tool, since it suggests objective comparability and quality. It is a simple number in which trust can be invested (Porter 1996) because it appears stripped from political and commercial narratives of persuasion. Yet that apparent stripping takes work: work that requires outside help. Similarly, health claims are not credible by default. Let us take a quick look at Unilever's "lowering cholesterol" claim about Flora proActiv margarine, and how it was made credible to food scientists, regulators, and potential consumers.

Scientists working in the food industry publish scores of scientific papers annually. They do so to strengthen their reputation in research, attract new scientists to their labs, and build prestige with partners, but also to disseminate data and claims meant to accompany (future) products. The readers of those papers are peer scientists, experts in food science, and often promising and desired collaborators. However, those peer scientists also perform another important role: they are the members of the expert panels invited by the European Food

Safety Authority (EFSA) to judge health claims.

Health claims are strictly regulated in Europe. EFSA invites its panel to issue a *scientific opinion* based upon the evidence presented by the applicant. This opinion is subsequently handed to European regulators to inform their policy decision. In practice, regulators tend to follow EFSA's scientific opinions, thus making it extremely valuable to food industry companies applying for permission to use a health claim.

Recently, such a panel of scientists judged the validity of "Question No. EFSA-Q-2008-085." The question was presented by Unilever and dealt with the effects of plant sterols on human cholesterol levels. The company proposed three formulations for its claim, one of which was "Plant sterols have been proven to lower/reduce blood cholesterol significantly. Blood cholesterol lowering has been proven to reduce the risk of (coronary) heart disease." The EFSA panel decided that none of the options was fully correct and decided that a different wording "reflects the scientific evidence" better: "Plant sterols have been shown to lower/reduce blood cholesterol. Blood cholesterol lowering may reduce the risk of (coronary) heart disease" (EFSA 2008:9). EFSA's scientists decided that the absence of human intervention studies warranted this reformulation.

Just like the Copernicus Institute, EFSA acts as a referee and provides legitimacy and credibility for specific claims, but also for the claimant, which was Unilever in this case. In DSM's case, their customers are other businesses, populated by experts. To Unilever, however, customers are consumers scattered around the globe. The quality of

scientific dossiers presented to an institution like EFSA is largely inaccessible to them, despite EFSA's efforts to communicate its decisions widely.

In other words, doing science, collecting evidence, and getting approval from EFSA generate credibility for scientists. Credibility for scientists, in this case, is only a means to build credibility with consumers, for they will have to make the purchase. However, mainstream food science is not particularly successful at establishing public credibility. Those who are winning in the public dietary credibility market are authors like Atkins or Agaston, who use case studies and stories rather than universal and scientific data (Shapin 2007). Flora proActive's marketers used the very same strategy in their advertising campaign. Unilever introduced the consumer to Karin Bloemen, a 50-year-old Dutch singer and comedian who learns, in a 20-second-long commercial, that during menopause her cholesterol levels rose. In a second commercial, she tries—to her satisfaction—Flora proActive, and lowers her cholesterol.[2]

These commercials are technologies of persuasion and credibility, crafting specific connections. In the first commercial, the issue of high cholesterol was connected to women in menopause, thus linking an issue to a specific public. In the second commercial, the issue and public are then connected to the food product. A decent spread of cases, each with its own spokesperson, makes a metaphorical extension possible from Karin Bloemen to ourselves, and thus to every European consumer.

These brief commercials contain scientific claims, as does Flora proActive's packaging. These claims are permitted by EFSA, but scientific claims

2   The campaign is summarized here: http://goo.gl/nLMlF2 (accessed May 20, 2014). The two commercials can be viewed online, the first at http://www.youtube.com/watch?v=LJDw1m st3YY, and the second at http://www.youtube.com/watch?v=wXpZNG ea9AE.

alone cannot build consumer credibility. Unilever needs Karin at least as much as its EFSA-approved numbers and figures.

Building credibility for sustainability and health claims is a complex endeavor requiring the participation of diverse individuals and institutions. It is a process in which science, regulation, and the market merge, and all institutions have their part to play. Fluid and unfinished claims are important within institutions to provide direction, priority, and to force decisions, as in the case with the LCAs at DSM. Validation of claims by independent "other" institutions, whether it be the Copernicus Institute or EFSA, solidifies fluid claims. It provides a formal regulatory or slightly less formal yet legitimate foundation for further actions: sales, distribution, and even storytelling. The narrative credibility building toward consumers also requires the involvement of key institutions—in this case celebrities—thereby joining fame and fact in the act of selling a tub of margarine to the public.

All of the above displays an infrastructure to support, compare, relate, and enable the act of building credibility. It shows a material and social infrastructure that stars people, tools, materials, and institutions, all geared toward one thing: translating uncertainties into credibilities.

DR. BART PENDERS is an assistant professor in biomedicine and society at Maastricht University's School of Public Health and Primary Care and a Network Fellow at Harvard University's Edmond J. Safra Center for Ethics (2013-14). He studies how claims and claimants garner credibility and the role of scientific integrity and public-private partnerships in these processes.

DR. STEVEN M. FLIPSE is Assistant Professor in Science Communication at the Delft University of Technology; his research focuses on the role of interaction in the responsible development and deployment of new and emerging technology based innovations.

REFERENCES

European Food Safety Authority (EFSA). 2008. "Scientific Opinion of the Panel on Dietetic Products Nutrition and Allergies on a Request from Unilever PLC/NV on Plant Sterols and Lower/reduced Blood Cholesterol, Reduced the Risk of (Coronary) Heart Disease." The EFSA Journal 781:1-12.

Flipse, S. M., and B. Penders. 2012. "Geloofwaardigheid op de markt [Credibility in the marketplace]." In Ingrediënten van geloofwaardigheid. Goed eten onder de loep [Ingredients of credibility. Good food in the spotlight], edited by B. Penders and F. Van Dam, 121-36. Amsterdam: BoomLemma.

Penders, B. and A. P. Nelis. 2011. "Credibility Engineering in the Food Industry: Linking Science, Regulation and Marketing in a Corporate Context." Science in Context 29(4):487-515.

Porter, T. M. 1996. Trust in Numbers: The Pursuit of Objectivity in Science and Public Life. Princeton, NJ: Princeton University Press.

Scholtens, B. 1997. "Hopborsten-pillen." De Volkskrant, February 8. Online archive at http://www.volkskrant.nl/vk/nl/2672/ Wetenschap-Gezondheid/archief/article/ detail/484171/1997/02/08/Hopborsten-pillen. dhtml.

Shapin, S. 2007. "Expertise, Common Sense, and the Atkins Diet." In Public Science in Liberal Democracy, edited by J. M. Porter and P. W. B. Phillips, 174-93. Toronto, Canada: University of Toronto Press.

Measuring Food

Food system activist **Anna Lappé** takes stock of the pieces in this issue.

IN A SHORT YOUTUBE VIDEO called "The Secret Life of Eggs," the retail giant Walmart tells the story of the egg. Well, more specifically, the eggs it sells. It turns out those fragile little orbs take enormous amounts of energy to produce. The video quantifies the water used, the feed fed, the fuel expended, and the packaging produced all to get those eggs onto the behemoth's shelves.

Needless to say, it's a lot. And, as the video goes on to explain, every year the company has to throw away 5 billion: all that energy ended up wasted as billions of eggs sit, cracked and uneaten, in dumpsters across the country.

Why? The Walmart video says it's because government regulation stipulates if just one egg is cracked, retailers must throw away the whole carton for food safety and traceability concerns. Government-imposed waste. But, the video explains, Walmart has innovated an "organic laser" identification system would now allow the company to track each individual egg versus a whole

Fascinating, except there is one thing wrong with this script: The government doesn't actually require grocery stores to throw away cartons of eggs...

carton, making it possible for the company to save billions of eggs a year.

Fascinating, except there is one thing wrong with this script: The government doesn't actually require grocery stores to throw away cartons of eggs, according to the US Department of Agriculture (USDA) and the US Food and Drug Administration (FDA) spokespeople I interviewed. In fact, when I asked the USDA about the video, the spokesperson I talked with explained that they'd contacted Walmart to ask them to correct the script.

What is true is that Walmart had been throwing away all those eggs for all these years. Not because the government made them do it, but because it was cost-effective for the company. Any of the other options available—sending the cartons back as a return, for instance—would have required time and a workforce trained in the food safety regulations. With the company's ideologically rigid fixation on cutting labor costs at all costs, those options were not on the table. So the eggs were

thrown out. With its glossy video, the company is taking credit—5 billion eggs of credit—for a change in corporate practice that they could have done a long time ago.

How do we measure? What do we count? Who's doing the counting and who's overseeing the measurements? All of these questions matter if we want to understand how any system works, especially a system as complex and far-reaching as our global food system. These are key questions if we want to assess the sustainability of a system, the impacts of going to scale, the efficiencies of infrastructure.

In "The Secret Lives of Corporate Food," Susanne Freidberg shares another example of a Walmart corporate video, this time "The Secret Life of Sliced Turkey." In her piece, Freidberg notes how the company applies a "life-cycle analysis" to the production of turkey. As numbers fly buy, viewers are presented with the illusion of sustainability: a turkey processor reduces water use by 50 million gallons a year, we hear. A packager is using 35 percent less cardboard, and 17,000 more trees are left standing in the forest. This kind of analysis "allows companies to say they have looked at the big picture," Friedberg notes, but in reality much of the story is still missing. Animal welfare, worker safety, biodiversity: much is, by the nature of this kind of analysis, not captured. But as Friedberg notes, "This scale of analysis is itself authoritative."

In Emily Yates-Doerr's excellent piece ("Refrigerator Units, Normal Goods"), she shows how measurement can mislead using the refrigerator as an example. Moving between her experience conducting interviews in Guatemala with a presentation of global public health professionals, she reminds us how indicators can mislead. A refrigerator is determined as the best proxy for progress by a global public health leader. Meanwhile, Yates-Doerr's real-world experience unseats the measurement: Yes, she sees refrigerators in low-income housing developments in Guatemala she visits, but the appliances aren't used for cooling or freezing. Without access to electricity, the families are using the appliances for storage, large and bulky storage.

How we display what we measure is just as important as measurement tools themselves. Whether it's warning labels on tobacco, rBST labeling on milk, or nutrition panel labeling on processed foods, the politics of labeling is indeed contentious. Manufacturers know that labeling shapes purchasing power. In Javiér Lezaun's piece, "Iconoclasm in the Supermarket," he explores how we label, or don't, genetically engineered foods. And he shows how grassroots activists use do-it-yourself labeling initiatives as a way to subvert the stranglehold the food industry has on labeling regimes.

Alison Fairbrother and David Schleifer ("The Fish at the Heart of the Food System") take on the little-told story of the lesser-known but oh-so-important fish, the menhaden. The fact that most of us are not counting its loss, much less have ever even heard of this all-important fish, is hugely significant. Fairbrother and Schleifer explain the vital role of this fish in healthy ocean ecosystems. The value of leaving these fish in the ocean? Approximately $11 billion. Despite the benefits of keeping them in their natural habitat, Omega Protein—the main supplier of menhaden in the US marketplace— uses the fish for swine, cattle, and fish feed as well as to supply the booming fish oil marketplace. (After the FDA allowed labeling claims about omega-3 fatty acids [the "good" fats], fish oil sales jumped from $100 million in 2001 to $1.1 billion a decade later.) The unregulated overfishing of these sea creatures means that their stocks are 95 percent depleted. If you eat fish, pork, beef, or chicken, or take a fish oil supplement, you're very likely a culprit in their decline. But without labeling, without measurement, few of us realize it.

As the authors for this *Limn* issue grapple with food system scale, efficiency, and sustainability, they cause us to reflect on who controls what we see, know, and hear. After I placed those calls to the USDA and FDA about the Walmart "Secret Life of Eggs" video, Walmart actually edited the script. In the new version, the government doesn't get the blame. Watch it now, and there's no mention of the fictional regulation implicated in the billions of eggs wasted annually. But it does make you wonder: who is holding the company accountable on the next script? ∎

ANNA LAPPÉ *is a national bestselling author, most recently of* Diet for a Hot Planet: The Climate Crisis at the End of Your Fork and What You Can Do About It *(Bloomsbury), and the cofounder of the Small Planet Institute and Real Food Media Project.*